ClearRevise®

AQA GCSE
English Literature

Illustrated revision and practice

Blood Brothers
By Willy Russell

Published by
PG Online Limited
The Old Coach House
35 Main Road
Tolpuddle
Dorset
DT2 7EW
United Kingdom

sales@pgonline.co.uk
www.clearrevise.com
www.pgonline.co.uk
2023

PREFACE

Absolute clarity! That's the aim.

This is everything you need to ace the question on *Blood Brothers* and beam with pride.
The content is laid out in a beautifully illustrated format that is clear, approachable and as concise and simple as possible.

The checklist on the contents pages will help you keep track of what you have already worked through and what's left before the big day.

We have included worked exam-style questions with answers. There are also exam-style questions at the end of the book. You can check your answers against those given on pages 59–60.

LEVELS OF LEARNING

Based on the degree to which you are able to truly understand a new topic, we recommend that you work in stages. Start by reading a short explanation of something, then try to recall what you've just read. This will have limited effect if you stop there but it aids the next stage. Question everything. Write down your own summary and then complete and mark a related exam-style question. Cover up the answers if necessary but learn from them once you've seen them. Lastly, teach someone else. Explain the topic in a way that they can understand. Have a go at the different practice questions – they offer an insight into how and where marks are awarded.

Design and artwork: Jessica Webb / PG Online Ltd

First edition 2023   10 9 8 7 6 5 4 3 2 1
A catalogue entry for this book is available from the British Library
ISBN: 978-1-910523-91-9
Copyright © PG Online 2023
All rights reserved
No part of this publication may be reproduced, stored in a retrieval system, or transmitted in any form or by any means without the prior written permission of the copyright owner.

Printed on FSC® certified paper by Bell and Bain Ltd, Glasgow, UK.

THE SCIENCE OF REVISION

Illustrations and words

Research has shown that revising with words and pictures doubles the quality of responses by students.[1] This is known as 'dual-coding' because it provides two ways of fetching the information from our brain. The improvement in responses is particularly apparent in students when they are asked to apply their knowledge to different problems. Recall, application and judgement are all specifically and carefully assessed in public examination questions.

Retrieval of information

Retrieval practice encourages students to come up with answers to questions.[2] The closer the question is to one you might see in a real examination, the better. Also, the closer the environment in which a student revises is to the 'examination environment', the better. Students who had a test 2–7 days away did 30% better using retrieval practice than students who simply read, or repeatedly reread material. Students who were expected to teach the content to someone else after their revision period did better still.[3] What was found to be most interesting in other studies is that students using retrieval methods and testing for revision were also more resilient to the introduction of stress.[4]

Ebbinghaus' forgetting curve and spaced learning

Ebbinghaus' 140-year-old study examined the rate at which we forget things over time. The findings still hold true. However, the act of forgetting facts and techniques and relearning them is what cements them into the brain.[5] Spacing out revision is more effective than cramming – we know that, but students should also know that the space between revisiting material should vary depending on how far away the examination is. A cyclical approach is required. An examination 12 months away necessitates revisiting covered material about once a month. A test in 30 days should have topics revisited every 3 days – intervals of roughly a tenth of the time available.[6]

Summary

Students: the more tests and past questions you do, in an environment as close to examination conditions as possible, the better you are likely to perform on the day. If you prefer to listen to music while you revise, tunes without lyrics will be far less detrimental to your memory and retention. Silence is most effective.[5] If you choose to study with friends, choose carefully – effort is contagious.[7]

---

1. Mayer, R. E., & Anderson, R. B. (1991). Animations need narrations: An experimental test of dual-coding hypothesis. *Journal of Education Psychology*, (83)4, 484–490.
2. Roediger III, H. L., & Karpicke, J.D. (2006). Test-enhanced learning: Taking memory tests improves long-term retention. *Psychological Science*, 17(3), 249–255.
3. Nestojko, J., Bui, D., Kornell, N. & Bjork, E. (2014). Expecting to teach enhances learning and organisation of knowledge in free recall of text passages. *Memory and Cognition*, 42(7), 1038–1048.
4. Smith, A. M., Floerke, V. A., & Thomas, A. K. (2016) Retrieval practice protects memory against acute stress. *Science*, 354(6315), 1046–1048.
5. Perham, N., & Currie, H. (2014). Does listening to preferred music improve comprehension performance? *Applied Cognitive Psychology*, 28(2), 279–284.
6. Cepeda, N. J., Vul, E., Rohrer, D., Wixted, J. T. & Pashler, H. (2008). Spacing effects in learning a temporal ridgeline of optimal retention. *Psychological Science*, 19(11), 1095–1102.
7. Busch, B. & Watson, E. (2019), *The Science of Learning*, 1st ed. Routledge.

CONTENTS

Assessment objectives .... vi ☑

Context, language and structure

Russell and *Blood Brothers* .... 2 ☐
Context .... 4 ☐
Features of plays .... 6 ☐
Language techniques .... 10 ☐

Analysis of acts

Act One .... 15 ☐
Act Two .... 23 ☐

Analysis of characters

Characters: Mrs Johnstone .... 31 ☐
Characters: Mrs Lyons .... 34 ☐
Characters: Mr Lyons .... 36 ☐
Characters: Mickey Johnstone .... 37 ☐
Characters: Edward Lyons .... 40 ☐
Characters: Linda .... 42 ☐
Characters: Sammy Johnstone .... 43 ☐
Characters: The Narrator .... 44 ☐

Analysis of themes

Themes: Social class .... 46 ☐
Themes: Friendship .... 49 ☐
Themes: Growing up .... 50 ☐
Themes: Fate and superstition .... 52 ☐
Themes: Gender .... 55 ☐
Examination practice **58**

Examination practice answers 59
Levels-based mark schemes for extended response questions 61
Index 63
Examination tips **65**

MARK ALLOCATIONS

All the questions in this book require extended responses. These answers should be marked as a whole in accordance with the levels of response guidance on **page 61**. The answers provided are examples only. There are many more points to make than there are marks available, so the answers are not exhaustive.

ASSESSMENT OBJECTIVES

In the exam, your answers will be marked against assessment objectives (AOs). It's important you understand which skills each AO tests.

AO1
- Show the ability to read, understand and respond to texts.
- Answers should maintain a critical style and develop an informed personal response.
- Use examples from the text, including quotes, to support and illustrate points.

AO2
- Analyse the language, form and structure used by a writer to create meanings and effects, using relevant subject terminology where appropriate.

AO3
- Show understanding of the relationships between texts and the contexts in which they were written.

AO4
- Use a range of vocabulary and sentence structures for clarity, purpose and effect, with accurate spelling and punctuation.

The AOs on this page have been written in simple language. See the AQA website for the official wording.

PAPER 2
Modern texts and poetry

Information about Paper 2

Written exam: 2 hours 15 minutes (this includes the questions on poetry)

96 marks (30 marks for modern texts plus 4 marks for SPaG, 30 marks for the poetry anthology and 32 marks for unseen poetry)

60% of the qualification grade (20% for modern texts, 20% for the poetry anthology and 20% for unseen poetry)

This guide covers the section on modern texts.

Questions
One extended-writing question on a modern text (you will be given a choice of two questions, but you should only answer one), one extended writing question on the poetry anthology you have studied and two questions on the unseen poems.

RUSSELL AND *BLOOD BROTHERS*

Blood Brothers is a play by Willy Russell which was first performed in 1983.

Willy Russell

Willy Russell (b. 1946) is an English playwright and composer. He was born near Liverpool into a working-class family. He left school aged 15 with one O Level (qualifications which were replaced with GCSEs) in English, and trained as a hairdresser before becoming a teacher.

Blood Brothers is set in and around Liverpool and the play draws on Russell's experiences.

Willy Russell

Russell began writing playscripts in the early 1970s, and has won awards for his plays *Educating Rita* and *Shirley Valentine*. Russell wrote *Blood Brothers* in the early 1980s, and it was first performed in Liverpool in January 1983. *Blood Brothers* has been performed consistently since the 1980s.

Comment: The popularity of *Blood Brothers* shows that it is still relevant today, 40 years after it was first written.

Blood Brothers

Musical

Blood Brothers is a musical: songs that were written by Russell are sung by the cast at key moments. The songs often help create a mood, for example, *Kids' Game*, is lively and upbeat. Some songs, such as *Marilyn Monroe*, reoccur several times with different lyrics.

Songs that are repeated at several points within a play are known as reprises. Reprises can show how characters have changed over the course of the play.

- The first time Mrs Johnstone sings *Marilyn Monroe*, she explains how she met her husband, and how he left her for another woman.
- The second time she sings *Marilyn Monroe* is at the start of Act Two, where she uses the song to describe her life in Skelmersdale and how her children have grown up.
- The third and final time Mrs Johnstone sings *Marilyn Monroe* is when Mickey has been diagnosed with depression and his doctor has prescribed him anti-depressants.

Comment: Marilyn Monroe is a recurring motif throughout the play. See **page 14**.

Some of the songs act as **soliloquies**, where characters express their inner feelings to the audience. One example is *Long Sunday Afternoon / My Friend*, where Mickey sings about his loneliness and how he misses Edward after he moves away. Other songs help to drive the plot forward, for example, Mr Lyons fires Mickey in the song *Take a Letter Miss Jones*.

Blood Brothers continued

Tragedy

Blood Brothers is an example of a tragedy: a genre of literature where the main characters meet an unhappy ending.

In a typical tragedy, a **protagonist** (main character) who is usually a member of the social elite, exhibits a **fatal flaw** (a characteristic that brings about their downfall). The character ends up being killed by an **antagonist** (the protagonist's rival).

In *Blood Brothers*, it could be suggested that Mickey is the protagonist, and that his working-class background is his fatal flaw.

> **Comment:** Mickey's working-class upbringing means he has little money and few opportunities, so he struggles when he loses his job. His financial worries cause him to take part in the robbery which contributes to his worsening mental health and addiction issues. At the end of the play, the Narrator hints that *"class"* is to blame for his death.

Mrs Lyons could be interpreted as the play's antagonist. She tells Mickey about Edward and Linda's affair which causes Mickey to threaten Edward with the gun that kills him, which in turn, causes the police officer to shoot Mickey.

The theme of fate (see **page 52**) suggests that the twins' deaths are unavoidable, but all the characters make decisions which contribute to the twins' tragic ending.

Blood Brothers shares other features with tragedies, such as starting the play with a prologue which summarises the play and reveals the ending. Prologues were often used in Greek tragedies to establish the characters and setting, as well as foreshadow events to come.

> **Comment:** In Greek tragedies, the prologue would be spoken by the chorus (a group of actors). In *Blood Brothers*, the Narrator (see **page 44**) fills the role of the chorus.

Comedy

There are lots of funny and light-hearted moments in *Blood Brothers*. This stops the play from being overwhelmingly sad and provides some comic relief for the audience.

 When the boys first meet, Mickey tells Edward that Sammy has a plate in his head. The boys mistakenly think it's *"little plates that you have bread off"*.

 Mickey tells his teacher that the African tribe eat *"Fish fingers"*.

 When the boys go to the cinema to see *Nymphomaniac Nights* and *Swedish Au Pairs*, they chant *"Tits, tits, tits"*.

Most of the funny moments happen in Act One and the start of Act Two. Once Mickey loses his job, the tone of the play becomes much more serious as the characters hurtle towards their tragic ending.

CONTEXT

The context of the 1960s, 70s and 80s are important for understanding the deeper meaning of the play.

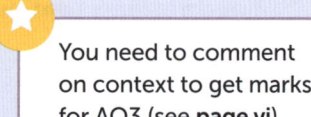

You need to comment on context to get marks for AO3 (see **page vi**).

Setting

Blood Brothers is set in the north-west of England, in Liverpool and Skelmersdale (a town north of Liverpool). The events of the play span the 1960s, 70s and 80s.

Comment: Russell wrote the play in the early 1980s, so he was influenced by what was happening in the UK at the time, including mass unemployment. See **page 5**.

Class

In Britain in the second half of the 20th century, families could be categorised into three social classes: upper, middle and working class. The class system was fixed, and it was difficult to move up the hierarchy.

Upper-class families were the richest members of society and belonged to the aristocracy (families with inherited land and wealth). Upper-class families probably made up about 5% of the population.

Middle-class families like the Lyonses had money, but they earned it through well-paid, professions, such as managerial roles. They accounted for approximately 15% of the population.

The rest of the population belonged to the working class, like the Johnstones. Working-class families made their livings through low-paid jobs and could struggle to make ends meet, with some families living in poverty.

A mother with three children in a Liverpool slum in 1962.

Comment: *Blood Brothers* explores the effect that social class has on a person's opportunities in life. For more on the theme of social class, see **page 46**.

Like most cities, Liverpool's population was made up of families from different social classes, and a person's social class dictated the quality of housing they lived in. For example, middle-class people lived in larger homes in more affluent neighbourhoods closer to green spaces, such as parks and fields. On the other hand, working-class people lived in more deprived, built-up areas in smaller, poorer quality housing.

From the 1940s, the government tried to tackle the issue of poor housing by designating **new towns** on the outskirts of cities. These new towns were supposed to have better amenities and give people more space than they had in the inner city. Skelmersdale, where both the Lyonses and Johnstones move to, was established as a new town in the 1960s.

Education

In the mid-twentieth century, a person's class often dictated the quality of education they received. At the end of primary school, children sat an exam which tested their academic ability. Students who scored highly went to grammar schools, while almost everyone else went to state schools. Grammar schools focused on academic subjects and prepared students for professional jobs, while state schools prepared students for manual labour (for boys) or homemaking (for girls).

Comment: In the play, Mickey and Linda attend a state school, whereas Edward attends a fee-paying private school. Mickey's education leads him to a job in the box factory and Linda becomes a housewife whereas Edward becomes a local councillor.

Many wealthy families recognised the importance of a grammar school education, so would pay for tutors or resources to help their child pass the entrance test. Working-class families often didn't have the money to give their children this advantage. As a result, far more upper- and middle-class children attended grammar schools than working-class children, and middle-class children who failed the entrance exam could attend fee-paying private schools instead. This meant upper- and middle-class students often had a greater chance of landing higher-paid jobs once they left school.

Comment: Some argued that this system restricted people's access to education, and trapped working-class people in menial jobs which prevented them from escaping poverty.

Employment

Liverpool's industry originally centred around shipbuilding and trade through its ports, but this began to decline by the second half of the twentieth century.

In the 1980s, the British Prime Minster, Margaret Thatcher, decided to close down some industries because they were no longer profitable. Industries such as mining and shipbuilding, which had employed thousands of working-class people, were forced to shut, and these people became unemployed. Many of these unemployed people only had experience in a particular industry, and had little education to help them find other work. The high levels of unemployment also meant there was a lot of competition for jobs, and many unemployed people were jobless for long periods of time.

Margaret Thatcher

The government attempted to help by providing unemployment benefits, known as the **dole**. These payments often weren't enough to adequately support a family. Financial worries often contributed to poor mental health, and many suffered from depression, used alcohol or drugs to help them cope, or were forced to commit crimes to make ends meet.

Comment: When Mickey is laid off from the factory, he spends months trying to find a new job. When he cannot find employment, he takes part in a robbery to make money.

The middle classes were less affected by the closure of British industries. Many middle-class workers were well educated or were more highly skilled which meant they could easily find work elsewhere.

Comment: Mr Lyons is unaffected by the layoffs at his factory, and Edward, who has a university degree, doesn't struggle to find a job.

FEATURES OF PLAYS

Plays are written to be performed, rather than read, so there are features in playscripts that are different to novels.

Acts and scenes

There are two **acts** in *Blood Brothers*. The first act spans about eight years: from a few months before the twins are born, up to them being nearly eight. There's a seven-year gap between Act One and Act Two. When Act Two starts, the twins are about 14, and ends when they are in their twenties.

Comment: Time speeds up at certain points in the play. For example, in Act Two, the twins age from 14 to 18 in a **montage** (a quick succession of short scenes). This represents how their carefree teenage years pass quickly.

There are no distinct scene changes within each act: the action shifts quickly and continuously between different characters.

Scene changes can be signalled by:

 characters entering or exiting the stage — after the policeman catches Mickey, Linda and Edward throwing stones, Mrs Johnstone enters the stage to show that the policeman has gone to visit the Johnstones' home.

 characters moving across the stage — the Johnstones walk across the stage with their suitcases to show their move from Liverpool to Skelmersdale.

 using props — the Narrator produces a *"listening funnel"* when he's playing the role of the gynaecologist to show that Mrs Johnstone is in hospital.

 sound effects — *"Christmas bells"* are used to signal that Edward is home from university in December.

 the Narrator — the Narrator's song *Shoes Upon the Table* links the scene where Mrs Johnstone is fired from her cleaning job to a new scene seven years later.

Structure

The play has a **cyclical structure**: it starts by revealing the ending. The Narrator summarises what will happen in the play during his **prologue**.

> **Comment:** The prologue rhymes, which reinforces its importance, and also creates an eerie atmosphere. It stands out from the informal, naturalistic dialogue used elsewhere in the play. For more on the Narrator's dialogue, turn to **page 10**.

The play begins with a re-enactment of the final scene, showing how Mickey and Edward die.

> **Comment:** Starting the play in this way suggests that the twins' fate is inevitable, and nothing can change their destinies. For more on the theme of fate, turn to **page 52**.

Following the prologue, the events of Acts One and Two are **chronological**, and the audience watches what happens from just before the twins are born, right up until their deaths.

Juxtaposed scenes

Some scenes are **juxtaposed** (deliberately put next to each other) so that the audience can directly compare them. Russell does this to contrast how the twins' different social classes affect their lives.

In Act One, Russell juxtaposes the scene where the police officer speaks with Mrs Johnstone about Mickey throwing stones with the scene where he speaks to the Lyonses. This allows the audience to see how the police officer blames Mickey and threatens Mrs Johnstone, but talks sympathetically to the Lyonses saying it was just a "*prank*". The police officer's harsh treatment of Mrs Johnstone shows how working-class people could be treated unfairly by society.

In Act Two, Russell juxtaposes the twins' experiences in school. Edward speaks respectfully to his teacher, calling him "*sir*" and his teacher suggests that Edward might be headed to "*Oxbridge*" (two prestigious English universities, Oxford and Cambridge).

In the following scene at Mickey's school, Mickey's teacher calls a student a "*turd*" and taunts Mickey when he doesn't know the answer to a question. This highlights the differences between students' experiences at school, and the quality of education the middle classes received compared to the working classes at the time.

> **Comment:** Despite their different experiences at school, both boys get suspended for being disrespectful to their teacher. This shows that regardless of their separate upbringings, the boys are alike in nature.

Simultaneous scenes

In Act Two, there is an example of a simultaneous scene (when two scenes are performed on the stage at the same time). Sammy (see **page 43**) convinces Mickey to be a lookout for the robbery while Edward tells Linda (see **page 42**) that he loves her.

Comment: Staging these two events simultaneously reinforces their importance to the rest of the play. Mickey's decision to participate in the robbery and Edward's love for Linda are pivotal plot points which contribute to the twins' downfall.

> While it's handy to memorise a few key quotations that you can use in the exam, it's also helpful to be able to identify pivotal moments in the play too.

Setting and props

Russell provides very little information in the stage directions (see **page 9**) about the play's set, how it should look and how it should be positioned. The production note suggests there should be *"the minimum of properties and furniture"* to allow the play to flow *"easily and smoothly"*.

Comment: A simple set means that the audience isn't distracted by the stagehands moving furniture and large props which allows the audience to focus on the story instead.

The only semi-permanent areas on stage are the interior of the Lyonses' house and the exterior of the Johnstones' house. Other scenes take place in the space between the two houses.

Mrs Johnstone with a pram.

Comment: Having both the Johnstones' house and the Lyonses' house on the stage at the same time is a visual reminder of how different their lifestyles are.

Props are used to help the action come to life. For example, Mrs Johnstone carries *"a brush, dusters and mop bucket"* to signal her cleaning job at the Lyonses' house, and she wheels a pram to signify that the twins have been born.

Stage directions

Stage directions are used to tell a director how the play should be performed and to guide the actors. Some stage directions tell actors when to enter or exit the stage or how to deliver a line, whereas other stage directions help to create a certain atmosphere or increase tension, for example, information about settings or sound effects.

| Mrs Johnstone is *"aged thirty but looks more like fifty"*. | **Comment:** This description suggests that Mrs Johnstone has aged prematurely because she's had a hard life. The play's costume department might show this through frumpy clothing or using make-up to make the actor seem older. |

| Mrs Lyons lives in *"comparative opulence"*. | **Comment:** The setting of the Lyonses' house should show that they live in wealth and comfort compared to the Johnstones. This could be shown using expensive-looking furniture to highlight the class division between the two families. |

| *A bass note, repeated as a heartbeat.* | **Comment:** Since the play is a musical, sound is very important. A heartbeat is heard when Mrs Johnstone swears on the Bible that she will give one of the twins to Mrs Lyons. The heartbeat mimics the women's pounding hearts suggesting both fear (Mrs Johnstone) and excitement (Mrs Lyons). It is also reminiscent of a baby's heartbeat during an ultrasound and reminds the audience of the twins who are impacted by the women's decision. |

| Mickey: *(suspiciously)* | **Comment:** When Mickey first meets Edward, he is suspicious. Mickey is used to other children teasing or bullying him, so he's wary of Edward. |

| Mrs Johnstone: *(screaming)* | **Comment:** When Mrs Lyons attacks Mrs Johnstone, Mrs Johnstone screams at Mrs Lyons. This heightens the tension and adds to the frenzied atmosphere of the scene. |

GCSE English Literature | Blood Brothers

LANGUAGE TECHNIQUES

The dialogue in *Blood Brothers* was written to sound natural.

Natural speech

Russell tries to reflect natural speech patterns to make his dialogue as realistic as possible. This makes the characters and the events of the play seem more believable to the audience.

The Narrator is an exception. His lines are often spoken in rhyming couplets which make them stand out from the other characters' dialogue. This emphasises his sinister and unsettling presence. For more on the Narrator, turn to **page 44**.

Russell mimics natural speech by using short (sometimes incomplete or single-word) sentences, pauses, repetition, conversational language and interruptions.

Russell uses a lot of ellipsis (...) in his dialogue. These represent pauses, and can show that a character is thinking or hesitating.

Mrs Johnstone: *"The shoes… the shoes…"*	**Comment:** Repetition is often found in natural speech as a person thinks about what they want to say. Russell uses it here to show Mrs Johnstone's shock.
Mrs Lyons: *"Oh… you mean you're superstitious?"*	**Comment:** 'Oh' is often used in natural speech to show surprise. This indicates that Mrs Lyons is surprised by Mrs Johnstone's superstitious behaviour.
Mrs Johnstone: *"I'll tell someone… I'll tell the police… I'll bring the police in an'…"*	**Comment:** Mrs Johnstone's speech tails off which is often something that happens in natural speech. Her incomplete dialogue also shows how powerless she feels trying to stand up to Mrs Lyons.
Mickey: *"But why —"* **Mrs Johnstone:** *"Just shut up."*	**Comment:** The long dash shows that Mickey's dialogue stops suddenly as Mrs Johnstone interrupts. This exchange shows a typical parent-child interaction as Mickey tries to argue with his mother, who shuts down the conversation.

Regional accent

A person's accent could signify which social class the speaker belonged to. Upper- and middle-class people tended to speak in standard English with an accent known as **received pronunciation** (a neutral accent, that doesn't belong to any particular geographical area). Working-class people often had strong regional accents.

Most of the characters (aside from the Lyonses) are from the working class, so they speak with a Liverpudlian accent (also known as a scouse accent). Russell shows this in the dialogue by using phonetic spellings, non-standard grammar and dialect words:

Mrs Johnstone: *"I'll have money comin' in an' I'll be able to pay y'"*

Comment: Russell uses apostrophes to show how characters often drop the final letter(s) off words like 'coming', 'and' and 'you' when they speak.

Sammy: *"by dinner time they was dead"*

Comment: The characters sometimes use non-standard grammar. Here, Sammy uses the non-standard 'was' instead of 'were'.

Mickey: *"Ta ra, Eddie"*

Comment: *"Ta ra"* is a phrase found in the Liverpudlian dialect which means 'goodbye'.

Mrs Johnstone: *"we've gorra pack"*

Comment: *"gorra"* is an example of a phonetic spelling. It mimics how Mrs Johnstone pronounces 'got to' in her accent.

Comment: The working-class characters swear more than Mr and Mrs Lyons. They use words like *"bleedin'"*, *"soddin'"* and *"bloody"*. When Edward swears in front of his mother, she tells him off for speaking *"filth"*.

This contrasts with Mrs Johnstone who not only swears herself, but also doesn't seem bothered when her children swear.

Mrs Johnstone speaks with a Liverpudlian accent whereas Mrs Lyons speaks in standard English.

GCSE English Literature | Blood Brothers

Standard English

The Lyons family use **standard English** (the version of English that people agree to be 'correct' and is taught in schools), and the actors would likely speak with either a very subtle Liverpudlian accent, or in received pronunciation (see **page 11**). Their dialogue tends to be more formal, and their language often includes more sophisticated words than the Johnstones.

Mrs Lyons: *"Doesn't one get piles when one's pregnant?"*

Comment: Mrs Lyons uses 'one' as a personal pronoun. This is a very formal way of speaking.

Edward: *"We have been undergoing a remarkable celluloid experience"*

Comment: Edward sometimes uses elevated language in his speech which reflects that he is well educated.

Mrs Lyons: *"Edward, I think we can forget the silly things that Mickey said"*

Comment: Mrs Lyons calls her son by his full name, rather than shortening it to 'Eddie' like Mickey does.

Childish dialogue

Comment: Adult actors play the twins when they are children, so Russell uses dialogue to convey the characters' youth to the audience.

When Mickey, Linda and Edward are seven, their language is simple and childish.

Mickey: *"Mam, we're playin' mounted police an' Indians. I'm a Mountie. Mam, mam…"*

Comment: Mickey's repetition of *"mam"* shows his excitement and enthusiasm. The reference to childhood games reminds the audience of his young age.

Edward: *"Is that your mummy?"*

Comment: The word *"mummy"* reminds the audience of Edward's youth.

Linda: *"… if y' dead, there's no school"*

Comment: Linda uses childish logic to comfort Mickey about death.

12 ClearRevise

Dramatic irony

Dramatic irony is a technique when the audience knows more than the characters. For example, when Edward shows Mrs Lyons his locket, Mrs Lyons mistakenly thinks the photo of Mickey is Edward. Edward corrects her, saying, *"I never looked a bit like Mickey"*. This is an example of dramatic irony because the audience knows that Mickey and Edward are twins, so they would be expected to look alike.

Comment: This example of dramatic irony creates humour, but also an element of tension, as the audience wonders whether Edward will discover his true identity.

Foreshadowing

Foreshadowing hints at something that will happen later in the play. It can be used to create tension or a sense of unease amongst the audience. For example, Sammy is often associated with guns, and the audience knows he steals from Linda's mum and Mickey when he is younger. This foreshadows the gunpoint robbery he commits later in the play.

Comment: Russell also uses foreshadowing throughout the play to emphasise the theme of fate and how the twins cannot escape their destinies.

Repetition

Particular lines are repeated throughout the play to emphasise their importance.

Mrs Johnstone: *"Never sure / Who's at the door / Or the price I'll have to pay."*	**Comment:** This line references the literal debts that Mrs Johnstone owes (to the milkman, catalogue man and debt collectors), but it also refers to the metaphorical debt of giving up Edward. This reminds the audience that Mrs Johnstone will have to face the consequences of her actions: the twins' deaths.
The Narrator: *"the devil's got your number"*	**Comment:** This line is metaphorical, but it suggests that the devil could contact Mrs Johnstone at any point to demand the death of the twins. Mentioning the devil also creates a sinister atmosphere.

Comment: Throughout the play, the Narrator describes how the devil gets closer and closer to the Johnstone family. Initially, the devil is described as *"walking past your door"*, then *"leanin' on your door"*. Eventually, he is *"runnin' right beside you"* and then *"callin' your number up today"*. This imagery creates the feeling that Mrs Johnstone is being chased and hounded by the devil and that her children's fates are inescapable.

GCSE English Literature | Blood Brothers

Imagery

The Narrator often uses **imagery** associated with bad luck, for example, a full moon, spilled salt, pavement cracks, a broken mirror. These references remind the audience of the inevitability of the play's tragic ending.

Motifs

A **motif** is a recurring symbol (a significant person, idea or object that represents a theme).

Marilyn Monroe

References to Marilyn Monroe reccur throughout the play. Monroe was a beautiful and successful movie star, who shot to fame in the 1950s. She suffered from various mental health issues, developed a prescription drug addiction, and tragically died of an overdose in 1962.

When Mrs Johnstone is young, Monroe represents glamour and sex appeal, but by the end of the play, Monroe's life has parallels with Mickey's, and she represents drug addiction, mental health issues, lost hope and an untimely death.

Marilyn Monroe

Dancing

The motif of characters dancing often accompanies references to Marilyn Monroe. At first, dancing symbolises freedom and happiness, for example, when Mrs Johnstone first meets her husband. However, by Act Two, the motif has become more sinister. Mrs Johnstone describes how Mickey's mind has *"gone dancing"*, a euphemism for his declining mental health.

Guns

Guns feature frequently throughout the play, but particularly in relation to Sammy:
- He steals Mickey's *"best"* gun.
- When he first appears on-stage, he has a *"gun in hand"* and points it at Edward and Mickey.
- He claims, *"I'm gonna get a real gun soon, I'm gonna get an air gun."*
- He sings *"I got y' / I shot y'"* during the song *Kids' Game*.

Comment: Sammy's association with guns and shooting foreshadows his armed robbery of the filling station in Act Two.

As children, Mickey, Edward and Linda play with toy guns. They take an air pistol into the park to shoot at targets, and they go to a rifle-range at the fair.

Comment: The twins are often linked to guns which foreshadows their deaths by shooting.

ACT ONE

Act One spans about eight years. It introduces Mrs Johnstone, a struggling single mother, who gives away one of her twins to the wealthy Mrs Lyons. The twins are raised separately but meet again when they are almost eight.

Act One

The play begins with the Narrator summarising the play.

Comment: The Narrator's opening lines act as a prologue and establishes the play as a tragedy. See **page 3** for more on tragedies.

He tells the audience about the Johnstone twins, and how one twin was kept by his mother, and the other twin was given away. He reveals that the twins didn't know they were related until the day they died.

Comment: The prologue is written in rhyme, which emphasises its importance, but also makes it seem sinister with its chant-like tone.

Mrs Johnstone is a struggling single mother.

There is a re-enactment of the final moments of play, showing how the twins die.

Comment: Showing the deaths of the twins reinforces the idea of fate, and that people cannot escape their destinies. For more on the theme of fate, see **page 52**.

The Narrator introduces Mrs Johnstone.

Comment: For most of the play, the other characters cannot see or hear the Narrator.

Mrs Johnstone recalls how she met her husband. As a young couple, they fell pregnant and got married. After having the baby, she fell pregnant again. Now Mrs Johnstone has seven children with an eighth on the way, and her husband has left her for another woman.

Comment: This song functions as a **soliloquy** which establishes Mrs Johnstone as a sympathetic character. She's a single mother raising seven children. The audience doesn't learn the names of most of Mrs Johnstone's children. This represents how society viewed working-class children as invisible.

The Narrator, dressed as a milkman, interrupts Mrs Johnstone's song.

Comment: The Narrator occasionally plays minor characters who interact with the main characters. The minor characters played by the Narrator tend to be unpleasant or deliver bad news. For more on the characters played by the Narrator, turn to **page 45**.

Act One continued

The Milkman demands payment for the Johnstones' overdue milk bill. Mrs Johnstone asks for an extension: she's starting a new job soon, so she'll be able to pay her debts next week.

Comment: Mrs Johnstone's dialogue uses apostrophes to show that she often doesn't pronounce letters at the end of words: *"I'll have money comin' in an' I'll be able to pay y'"*. This conveys her Liverpudlian accent. For more on regional accents, turn to **page 11**.

The Milkman exits, and Mrs Johnstone is left alone on stage. Four of her children are heard calling for her off-stage: *"Mam, Mam, the baby's cryin'"*.

Comment: Positioning Mrs Johnstone alone on stage while her children call for her reinforces how she has been abandoned by her husband and how she is responsible for raising a large family by herself. This creates sympathy for Mrs Johnstone.

Mrs Johnstone's children claim they are *"hungry"* and *"starvin'"*.

Comment: It's clear from the outset that the Johnstone family are barely scraping by, and don't have enough to eat. This conveys the difficulties faced by working-class families and helps to explain why Mrs Johnstone chooses to give up one of the twins later.

Mrs Johnstone goes to Mrs Lyons' house, where she has a new job as a cleaner. Russell creates an obvious class divide between Mrs Lyons and Mrs Johnstone.
- Mrs Lyons complains that her house is too big for just her and her husband, whereas Mrs Johnstone is cramped inside a small house with seven children.
- Mrs Lyons speaks in standard English, whereas Mrs Johnstone speaks with a regional accent.
- Mrs Lyons enters the stage carrying a parcel (which is revealed to contain a new pair of shoes), whereas Mrs Johnstone can't afford to pay her milk bill.
- Mrs Lyons can afford to employ Mrs Johnstone to clean her house.

Comment: This establishes another power divide between the two women, where one is an employer, and one is an employee.

Mrs Lyons tells Mrs Johnstone that her husband has been away on business for the past four months, and she's been living in the house alone. She admits that she has been unable to have children of her own.

Comment: This creates sympathy for Mrs Lyons. She is presented as lonely and unhappy. For more on the character of Mrs Lyons, turn to **page 34**.

Mrs Lyons opens her parcel and puts a pair of new shoes on the table. Mrs Johnstone is shocked: she believes that putting new shoes on a table will bring bad luck.

Comment: It's important that Mrs Johnstone is established as a superstitious character. The superstition Mrs Lyons invents about parted twins dying prevents Mrs Johnstone from ever telling her sons the truth. For more on superstition, turn to **page 52**.

16 Clear**Revise**

Act One continued

The scene changes and Mrs Johnstone visits a gynaecologist (played by the Narrator) who tells her that she's expecting twins. Mrs Johnstone is *"numbed"*: she can't afford to raise another child.

> **Comment:** Mrs Johnstone's despair about providing for another child explains why she agrees to give away one of the twins: she's in a hopeless situation.

Mrs Johnstone is back cleaning at Mrs Lyons'. Mrs Johnstone tells Mrs Lyons that she's expecting twins. Mrs Lyons asks Mrs Johnstone to give her one of the twins, and exploits Mrs Johnstone's fears about being unable to raise another child.

> **Comment:** Mrs Lyons' dialogue is forceful. She says, *"Quickly, quickly"*, rushing Mrs Johnstone, and uses **rhetorical questions** ("*how can you possibly avoid some of them being put into care?*") to convince Mrs Johnstone she couldn't cope with another child.

Mrs Lyons intends to fake a pregnancy until the twins are born. Her husband returns from his business trip after the babies are due, so he would never suspect the child wasn't his. Mrs Johnstone recognises that a child raised by the Lyonses would have a better quality of life than she could provide. Mrs Lyons promises that Mrs Johnstone would still be able to see her child when she visits the Lyonses' house to clean. Mrs Johnstone eventually agrees to give up one of the twins. Mrs Lyons makes Mrs Johnstone swear on the Bible.

Mrs Johnstone decides to give one of the twins away.

> **Comment:** The Narrator says, *"In the name of Jesus, the thing was done, / Now there's no going back, for anyone"*. This reinforces how the characters' fates have been sealed.

The play fast-forwards to five months later, and Mrs Johnstone has given birth. As Mrs Johnstone leaves the hospital, she is confronted by *"Various debt collectors"* who demand payment for items that she has bought on credit.

> **Comment:** Mrs Johnstone buys things on credit, knowing she won't be able to pay for them. This presents her as an irresponsible character who doesn't think about the long-term consequences of her actions.

As the debt collectors repossess items from the house, Mrs Johnstone sings: *"Only mine until / The time comes round / To pay the bill"*.

> **Comment:** Just like the furniture Mrs Johnstone bought on credit, she knows that she'll have to give up one of the twins too.

Mrs Johnstone visits Mrs Lyons, who is irritated that Mrs Johnstone didn't tell her that the babies had been born. She forces Mrs Johnstone to hand over one of the twins: *"I must have my baby"*.

> **Comment:** Mrs Lyons doesn't recognise how hard it is for Mrs Johnstone to give up one of the twins. Mrs Lyons is only concerned with getting what she wants.

Act One continued

Mrs Lyons picks one of the twins and tells Mrs Johnstone she can have the week off from cleaning.

Comment: Mrs Lyons had promised Mrs Johnstone that she could see the other twin all the time, but she's already starting to go back on her promise. This hints at Mrs Lyons' manipulative personality: she doesn't care about Mrs Johnstone now she's got the baby.

Mrs Johnstone returns home, and her children ask what happened to the other twin. Mrs Johnstone tells them that he has *"gone up to heaven"*.

The children pester Mrs Johnstone for toys and clothes, and Mrs Johnstone says: *"I'll have a look in the catalogue"*.

Comment: Mrs Johnstone hasn't learned from her mistakes: she still intends to order things she can't afford.

A week later, Mrs Johnstone returns to work at the Lyonses'. She looks in the cot, *"beaming and cooing"* at baby Edward. Mrs Lyons is *"agitated"* by the attention Mrs Johnstone is giving to the baby.

Comment: This introduces the paranoia that Mrs Lyons feels for the remainder of the play: she is terrified that Mrs Johnstone will take Edward back.

Mrs Lyons tells Mrs Johnstone to get back to work, and Mrs Johnstone exits.

Mr Lyons tells Mrs Lyons, *"don't be hard on the woman. She only wanted to hold the baby"*. Mrs Lyons replies: *"I don't want her to hold the baby... I don't want the baby to catch anything"*.

Comment: Mrs Lyons implies that Mrs Johnstone is dirty. This shows her class prejudice.

Mrs Lyons complains to her husband that Mrs Johnstone is always *"bothering"* the baby and that she *"ignores"* her work. Mrs Lyons decides to fire Mrs Johnstone. Mr Lyons agrees saying: *"I suppose you know best. The house is your domain"*.

Comment: This exchange reinforces stereotypical gender roles. As a woman, Mrs Lyons is responsible for looking after the home and the baby. For more on the theme of gender, turn to **page 55**.

Mrs Lyons asks her husband for £50 for *"things to buy for the baby"*, and he gives her the money.

Mr Lyons leaves, and Mrs Lyons calls Mrs Johnstone back on stage. Mrs Lyons fires Mrs Johnstone, claiming her cleaning has *"deteriorated"*.

> £50 is equivalent to about £1,000 today.

Comment: The audience recognises that Mrs Lyons is actually firing Mrs Johnstone because she is jealous of Mrs Johnstone being near the baby. Mrs Lyons is already breaking her promise that Mrs Johnstone could see the baby *"every day"*.

Act One continued

Mrs Lyons gives the £50 to Mrs Johnstone. Mrs Johnstone threatens to take her son back and tell the police that Mrs Lyons has her child. Mrs Lyons tells Mrs Johnstone that the police would send her to prison for giving up her baby. Mrs Lyons exploits Mrs Johnstone's superstitious nature and invents a superstition: *"if either twin learns that he was once a pair, they shall both immediately die"*.

Comment: Mrs Lyons manipulates those around her. She lies to her husband about her intentions for the £50, and she takes advantage of Mrs Johnstone's superstitious nature and love for the twins to get what she wants.

Mrs Johnstone takes the money and leaves the house.

The Narrator sings *Shoes Upon the Table*, a song with the lyrics, *"the devil's got your number, / Y' know he's gonna find y'"*.

Comment: This creates an ominous atmosphere and reminds the audience that the Johnstone twins are fated to die.

The play fast-forwards seven years. Mrs Johnstone's twin, Mickey, has been playing outside. He's upset because his elder brother, Sammy, has *"robbed me other gun"*.

Mrs Johnstone is a loving mother.

Comment: Guns feature multiple times in the play. This foreshadows how the twins are shot at the end of the play. For more on guns, see **page 14**.

Mickey tells his mother that he has been playing near the *"big houses"* which makes Mrs Johnstone agitated.

Comment: Mrs Johnstone doesn't want Mickey playing near the *"big houses"* because that's where the Lyonses' live. She doesn't want Mickey to run into his twin, Edward.

Mickey sings a song about Sammy which presents Sammy as a naughty child: he steals his brother's toys, spits in people's eyes, and wees through people's letterboxes.

Comment: Even though the audience hasn't met Sammy yet, it's clear that he's a naughty child. Since Sammy is older, Mickey admires Sammy's bad behaviour.

Edward approaches Mickey and tells him that he's noticed him playing near the big houses. Edward gives Mickey some sweets.

Comment: Edward's dialogue is in standard English, and he uses formal, middle-class vocabulary like *"smashing"* and *"super"*. This contrasts with Mickey who speaks with a regional accent and uses swear words like *"bleedin'"*, *"Pissed"* and the *"'F' word"*. The difference in their dialogue illustrates the class division between the boys.

Act One continued

Mickey and Edward discover they have the same birthday, which Mickey says makes them *"blood brothers"*. They make a cut in their hands and shake.

Mrs Johnstone enters, and Mickey introduces Edward as his brother.

> **Comment:** The audience recognises the dramatic irony of Mickey and Edward being *"blood brothers"*. This heightens the tension, as they wonder if Mrs Johnstone will reveal the truth.

Mickey and Edward make a pact to be blood brothers.

Mrs Johnstone tells Mickey to go inside and tells Edward, *"Don't you ever come round here again."*

> **Comment:** Although Mrs Johnstone's reaction seems harsh, she is trying to protect Edward because she believes the boys will die if they discover that they are separated twins.

Edward goes home and the doorbell rings. Mickey appears, asking if Edward wants to play. Edward tells his mother that he and Mickey are blood brothers. Just like Mrs Johnstone, Mrs Lyons is horrified and escorts Mickey out of her house.

> **Comment:** Even though both Mrs Johnstone and Mrs Lyons try to keep the boys apart, they defy their mothers to become close friends. This suggests that the twins are destined to be in each other's lives. For more on the theme of fate, turn to **page 52**.

Mrs Lyons wants to know how Edward met Mickey, because she told him, *"never to go where that boy— where boys like that live"*.

> **Comment:** Mrs Lyons tells Edward that he's *"not the same"* as Mickey. She's reinforcing class prejudices by implying middle-class families are better than working-class families. For more on the theme of social class, turn to **page 46**.

Upset, Edward tells Mrs Lyons that he hates her, and he swears at her. Mrs Lyons hits Edward and tells him, that he has learnt *"filth"* from Mickey.

> **Comment:** Mrs Lyons' paranoia makes her aggressive. This foreshadows her escalating violence when she threatens Mrs Johnstone with a knife in Act Two.

Edward stands in his garden, and watches Mickey, Sammy, and a girl called Linda, playing. The children play several games where they are gangsters, cowboys, and soldiers. If a child 'dies' during the game, *"you count from one to ten, / You can get up off the ground again"*.

> **Comment:** The game represents the innocence of childhood, but it also foreshadows Mickey and Edward dying at the end of the play. However, unlike their childhood games, they don't *"get up off the ground again"*. For more on the theme of growing up, turn to **page 50**.

Act One continued

During the game, Mickey swears, and Sammy and the other children taunt him, telling him he will go to hell for swearing. Linda defends Mickey and threatens to tell her mother that Sammy has been stealing her mother's cigarettes and money.

> **Comment:** Linda subverts typical female stereotypes: she defends Mickey from the other children and stands up to Sammy. For more on the character of Linda, turn to **page 42**.

Mickey is upset by the taunts and tells Linda, *"I don't wanna die"*. Linda tells him, *"When you die you'll meet your twinny again"*.

> **Comment:** This is an example of dramatic irony because the audience knows that Mickey has already met his twin brother. It's also an example of foreshadowing: Mickey dies when he finds out Edward is his twin.

Mickey and Linda go to Edward's house and convince him to sneak out and play with them.

> **Comment:** Mickey and Linda offer Edward freedom from his strict home life.

Mrs Lyons realises that Edward has snuck out, and she is upset. She pleads with her husband to let them move away from Liverpool because she's worried about Edward mixing with the wrong crowd and drawing Edward away from her.

> **Comment:** Mrs Lyons' paranoia about Edward discovering his real mother has made her possessive and controlling.

Mr Lyons places a pair of shoes on the table, and Mrs Lyons *"sweeps"* them off.

> **Comment:** This highlights Mrs Lyons' growing insecurity: she's trying to avoid anything that might bring bad luck, even if it's an irrational superstition.

The scene changes to Mickey, Edward and Linda firing an airgun. The children then decide to throw stones at a nearby building. Just as they are about to throw the stones, a policeman catches them.

> **Comment:** Mickey and Linda act tough, but they burst into tears when they're caught by the policeman. This reminds the audience of their youth: they're scared of getting into trouble.

The policeman visits Mrs Johnstone to tell her he's caught the children. The policeman calls her *"missis"* (Mrs) and threatens her with *"the courts... or worse"*.

> **Comment:** The policeman treats Mrs Johnstone harshly because she's working class, and because of Sammy's previous run-ins with the law.

The policeman then visits the Lyonses. He speaks to Mr Lyons respectfully, calling him *"sir"*. The policeman says that it was probably just a *"prank"* and advises Edward not to *"mix with the likes of them"*.

> **Comment:** The way the policeman treats Mrs Johnstone compared to Mr and Mrs Lyons shows his class prejudice.

GCSE English Literature | Blood Brothers

Act One continued

The visit from the policeman convinces Mr Lyons that his family should move away from Liverpool.

Edward visits the Johnstones' house to tell them he's moving away. Mrs Johnstone gives Edward a locket with a picture of her and Mickey inside as a keepsake but tells him to keep it a secret.

> **Comment:** Mrs Johnstone comforts Edward when he's upset about moving house. She *"Cradles him, letting him cry"*. Unlike Mrs Lyons who is presented as a strict and overbearing mother, Mrs Johnstone is warm and loving.

Mrs Johnstone gives Edward a locket.

The scene changes to Edward and Mrs Lyons in their new home. Edward is despondent.

> **Comment:** Mrs Lyons wants to keep Edward and Mickey apart, but this upsets Edward, and causes him to resent her.

The scene shifts to Mickey who sings *Long Sunday Afternoon / My Friend*. The lyrics describe how much Mickey misses Edward.

> **Comment:** Edward joins in for a chorus of the song. This highlights the twins' bond.

Mrs Johnstone appears and tells Mickey that they're moving to Skelmersdale.

> Skelmersdale was a **new town**: a town designated to alleviate overcrowding in Liverpool. For more on new towns, see page 4.

Mrs Johnstone believes that moving to Skelmersdale will give her a fresh start: *"We're leavin' this mess / For our new address"*. She romanticises what life in Skelmersdale will be like: *"the garden's so big, / It would take you a week just to reach the far side."*

> **Comment:** Mrs Johnstone uses **hyperbole** (exaggeration, pronounced *hy-per-bol-ee*) to describe the size of the garden. This emphasises how optimistic and excited she feels.

When they arrive in Skelmersdale, Sammy immediately climbs on a cow.

> **Comment:** This is a moment of comic relief, but it also hints that the move to Skelmersdale won't necessarily change the family for the better.

Act One ends on a positive note, with the Johnstones excited about their new life in Skelmersdale.

> **Comment:** The audience may suspect that the Johnstones have moved to the same place as the Lyonses. This increases the tension as the audience suspects that the families' paths will cross again, reinforcing the idea that the twins are fated to be in each other's lives.

ACT TWO

Act Two begins about eight years after the end of Act One. The twins are now fourteen, and their paths cross once again. As the boys grow older, it becomes clear that Edward has benefitted from his middle-class upbringing.

Act Two

Act Two begins with the Johnstones in Skelmersdale. Some things seem positive: the house is *"lovely"*, Mrs Johnstone can pay her milk bill and she's been *"dancing"* with the milkman. But there are hints that not everything is perfect. Their neighbours *"fight"* and Sammy *"burnt the school down"*.

Comment: Mrs Johnstone doesn't blame Sammy for burning the school down and says *"it's very easily done"*. Instead, she blames the school for letting him play with *"magnesium"*. This shows how Mrs Johnstone doesn't take responsibility for her children's actions.

Mrs Johnstone says that her daughter, Donna Marie, has had three children.

Comment: This hints that Donna Marie's life could end up being very similar to Mrs Johnstone's, and suggests how difficult it can be for working-class women to escape the cycle of poverty.

The scene shifts to Mrs Lyons helping Edward pack to go to boarding school. She asks him: *"We're safe here, aren't we?"*

Comment: Even after 14 years, Mrs Lyons is still paranoid that someone will take Edward away from her.

The scene changes to Mrs Johnstone hurrying Mickey out of the house and on to the school bus. Linda is waiting for Mickey at the bus stop.

Comment: It's hinted that Mickey has feelings for Linda. Mrs Johnstone teases Mickey for talking about Linda in his sleep. Mickey and Linda's relationship is a key part of Act Two.

Sammy also gets on the bus because he's going to *"The dole"*.

Comment: Sammy doesn't have a job and is claiming unemployment benefit. For more about the dole, turn to **page 5**.

The bus pulls up, and the Narrator is playing the role of the bus conductor. He tells Mrs Johnstone that *"No one gets off without the price bein' paid"*.

Comment: This line has a dual meaning. It means that passengers must pay a fare to ride the bus, but it's also ominous. It suggests that Mrs Johnstone will pay the price for giving Edward away, reminding the audience about the twins' fate.

GCSE English Literature | Blood Brothers

Act Two continued

Mickey, Linda and Sammy get on the bus. Sammy tries to buy a *"fourpenny scholar"* (a bus ticket for passengers aged 14 and younger), but the conductor refuses, telling Sammy that he's too old. When Sammy argues back, the bus conductor tells the driver to drive to the police station. Mickey panics and tries to defend Sammy (*"He didn't mean it, mister"*) and offers to pay part of Sammy's bus fare.

> **Comment:** Even though Sammy bullied him as a child, Mickey defends Sammy, showing his loyalty to his older brother.

Sammy robs the bus conductor at knifepoint.

> **Comment:** Sammy's behaviour has escalated. He was naughty as a child, but now he's a violent criminal. For more on the character of Sammy, turn to **page 43**.

Linda prevents Mickey from getting involved, telling him: *"You stay where y' are, Mickey. You've done nothin'"*. She warns him: *"You better hadn't do anything soft, like him"*.

> **Comment:** Just like when they were younger, Linda protects Mickey. She tries to prevent him from making poor choices.

Linda tells Mickey, *"I don't care who knows. I just love you."*

> **Comment:** Linda subverts gender stereotypes by being vocal about her feelings for Mickey. However, she conforms to stereotypes by not asking him out herself: she expects Mickey to begin the relationship. For more on the theme of gender, turn to **page 55**.

The scene shifts to Edward's school. The Narrator is playing the role of Edward's teacher. The teacher accuses Edward of wearing a locket. The teacher demands that Edward give him the locket, but Edward refuses and swears at him. Edward is suspended from school.

> **Comment:** This shows Edward's loyalty. Mrs Johnstone asked Edward to keep the locket a secret, so he refuses to show his teacher, even though he gets into trouble.

The scene moves to Mickey and Linda in school. Mickey hasn't been paying attention, and he can't answer the teacher's question. Mickey and Linda misbehave, and they both get suspended.

> **Comment:** Russell juxtaposes the two classroom scenes to highlight the difference between the boys' educations. See **page 7** for more.

The scene switches to Edward at home with Mrs Lyons. She's found out he's been suspended because of his locket. Mrs Lyons opens the locket, and sees the picture of Mrs Johnstone and Mickey. Mrs Lyons mistakes the picture of Mickey for a picture of Edward, and demands, *"when were you photographed with this woman?"*. Edward refuses to tell Mrs Lyons about the locket, telling her: *"It's just a secret, everybody has secrets, don't you have secrets?"*

> **Comment:** This is an example of **dramatic irony**. The audience knows that Mrs Lyons is keeping a big secret from Edward.

Act Two continued

The scene changes to Mickey and Linda walking across a field. Linda tries flirting with Mickey, but he's too embarrassed to flirt back. Mickey points to a boy standing in his window. Linda tries to make Mickey jealous by saying *"He's lovely lookin'"*, but Mickey doesn't react, so she storms off.

Edward appears at the side of the stage, and Mickey notices him. They don't recognise each other right away, and they sing *That Guy*: a song about how they wish they looked like the other.

> **Comment:** The song is comedic in places: Mickey says his hair is the *"colour of gravy"* and Edward thinks he has *"halitosis"* (bad breath). It's ironic that Mickey and Edward both wish they were more like each other because they don't know that they're twins.

Mickey and Edward eventually recognise each other, and decide to go to the cinema.

> **Comment:** Even though they've been separated for almost eight years, they instantly rekindle their friendship. This highlights the strong bond they have as twins. For more on the theme of friendship, turn to **page 49**.

The twins meet again when they're 14.

Mrs Lyons watches the twins from a distance.

> **Comment:** Mrs Lyons is so paranoid about the Johnstones that she's secretly started following Edward. This emphasises her increasingly fragile mental state.

Mickey takes Edward to his house so that he can get some money for the cinema. After the boys leave, Mrs Lyons enters the Johnstones' house, having followed Mickey and Edward. Mrs Lyons accuses Mrs Johnstone of moving to Skelmersdale to be closer to Edward.

> **Comment:** Mrs Lyons' dialogue uses a lot of exclamation marks which signifies her agitation: *"Don't lie! I know what you're doing to me!"*

Mrs Lyons offers Mrs Johnstone *"thousands"* to move away from Skelmersdale, but Mrs Johnstone refuses saying, *"I don't want your money. I've made a life out here."*

> **Comment:** Mrs Johnstone has become more self-aware. She doesn't want Mrs Lyons' money because she'll only spend it on *"junk and trash"*: she knows that she's financially irresponsible. This also marks a power shift in the relationship between Mrs Johnstone and Mrs Lyons: Mrs Lyons can no longer control Mrs Johnstone with money.

Mrs Lyons picks up a kitchen knife and attacks Mrs Johnstone. Mrs Johnstone is able to defend herself and disarm Mrs Lyons.

> **Comment:** Mrs Lyons' paranoia has made her irrational and violent. She's prepared to do whatever she can to stop Mrs Johnstone from being involved in Edward's life, and this is a hint of further violence to come.

GCSE English Literature | Blood Brothers

Act Two continued

The scene switches to Mickey and Edward leaving the cinema, where they bump into Linda.

The Narrator enters, and performs a monologue which narrates Mickey, Edward and Linda's friendship over the course of the next four years, showing them on day trips to the fairground and the beach.

Edward, Linda and Mickey at the fairground.

Comment: The **montage** suggests their teenage years pass by quickly because they are carefree and happy.

Despite their happy teenage years, the Narrator's language has an ominous undertone. He comments that Mickey, Linda and Edward, *"don't even notice broken bottles in the sand"*.

Comment: This image suggests that the trio are destined to be hurt by something hidden. This reminds the audience that their happiness won't last because the twins are fated to die.

Linda, Mickey and Edward are now 18. Edward tells Linda he is miserable because he's leaving to go to university and he's going to miss her and Mickey.

Comment: Edward going to university reminds the audience of his middle-class privilege. This contrasts with Mickey who has a job at the box factory after leaving school.

Linda tells Edward that Mickey still hasn't asked her out. Edward confesses: *"If I was Mickey I would have asked you years ago"*. Edward then sings *I'm Not Saying a Word*, where he imagines how he would treat Linda if they were a couple: *"I'd just tell you that I love you / If it was me."*

Comment: Edward has feelings for Linda, but doesn't tell her because of his loyalty to Mickey.

Mickey enters, and Edward convinces him to ask Linda out. Mickey nervously asks Linda to be his girlfriend and she agrees.

Comment: This scene symbolises the end of childhood. Edward is off to university and Mickey and Linda have finally started a romantic relationship.

The play fast-forwards to a few months later. Mickey is at home, getting ready to go to work. He reveals to Mrs Johnstone that Linda is pregnant and they plan to get married in a month's time.

Comment: Linda's life is starting to mirror Mrs Johnstone's, showing how easily women are trapped in the cycle of working-class poverty.

At the time the play is set, it was expected that if a couple fell pregnant, they would get married before the baby arrived.

The scene changes to the wedding day, and Mickey wears his *"working clothes"* to the ceremony.

Comment: This implies that Mickey can't afford a suit for his wedding and symbolises how he cannot escape his working-class life.

... Act Two continued

Mr Lyons enters the stage and sings *Take a Letter Miss Jones*. In it, Mr Lyons dictates letters to his secretary, Miss Jones, telling workers that they have been laid off. During the song, Mickey is handed a letter, signalling he's been fired.

Mickey and other workers with their unemployment letters.

> **Comment:** This song marks a turning point in Mickey's life. Prior to this, he's employed, with a wife he loves and a baby on the way. Now he's unemployed with no means to support his family.

Mickey joins a dole queue with a group of other men.

> **Comment:** The long queue shows the high levels of unemployment in the 1970s–80s caused by the government's closure of unprofitable industries. See **page 5** for more.

Mickey is especially affected by losing his job. He's *"dejected"* and looks *"old before his time"*.

> **Comment:** Mickey being *"old before his time"* reminds the audience of Mrs Johnstone, who was described as *"aged thirty but looks more like fifty"*. This suggests that working-class people often looked older due to the hardships they faced.

The action fast-forwards three months, and Edward comes home from university for Christmas. Edward tells Mickey how *"fantastic"* his life is: he goes to parties and meets lots of new people.

> **Comment:** Edward is still enjoying his youth, whereas Mickey is struggling with his responsibilities. For more on the theme of growing up, turn to **page 50**.

Mickey isn't excited to see Edward and is unimpressed by his stories about university life.

> **Comment:** Mickey's dialogue shows his lack of enthusiasm. His lines are short and blunt: *"Nothin'. How's university?"*, *"Good."*, *"She's OK."*

Mickey eventually tells Edward that he's unemployed and has been *"walking around all day, every day, lookin' for a job"*.

> **Comment:** Mickey doesn't tell Edward that he's married Linda and that they're expecting a baby. This shows how the twins have drifted apart and Mickey no longer feels close to Edward.

Edward asks, *"why is a job so important?"*, and tells Mickey to *"live like a bohemian"*.

> **Comment:** Edward's comments are insensitive. He romanticises unemployment by comparing it to the bohemian lifestyle (a socially unconventional way of life, often associated with the arts). Edward doesn't understand that Mickey needs a job to survive.

Mickey is angry at Edward and tells him to *"beat it before I hit y'"*.

> **Comment:** This marks a turning point in Mickey and Edward's relationship. It's clear that class differences have altered the course of their lives.

GCSE English Literature | Blood Brothers

Act Two continued

The scene then splits with two interactions happening simultaneously. Edward talks with Linda, and Sammy talks with Mickey.

Comment: Russell stages both scenes simultaneously to emphasise their importance to the outcome of the play. It also increases the pace of the action, showing that the twins' rush into poor decisions which contribute to their downfall.

Edward tells Linda that he has *"always loved"* her. Linda tells Edward that she has *"always loved [him], in a way"* but that she's married to Mickey and expecting his baby.

Comment: Edward confessing his love for Linda foreshadows their affair.

Meanwhile, Sammy asks Mickey to be a lookout for him during a robbery. Sammy promises Mickey *"Fifty quid for an hour's work"*, and Mickey agrees.

Mickey tells Linda that he's been offered a job, and he'll buy her a *"slap-up meal"* and *"new clothes"*.

Comment: Just like Mrs Johnstone, Mickey is financially irresponsible. He intends to spend his money on frivolous things.

Linda suspects that Mickey is going to do something illegal to earn the money, and tries to stop him, but he walks away.

Sammy and Mickey during the robbery.

Comment: This marks a shift in Linda and Mickey's relationship. When they were 14, Linda was able to stop Mickey from getting involved with Sammy's bus robbery, but now, she can't prevent Mickey from making bad decisions.

The scene shifts to Mickey keeping a lookout while Sammy robs an offstage character, threatening him with a gun. An alarm sounds, and Sammy shoots. Sammy and Mickey flee the scene. They run to Mrs Johnstone's house, and Sammy hides the gun under the floorboards.

Comment: The gun Sammy hides under the floorboards is the same weapon Mickey uses to shoot Edward at the end of the play.

Mickey and Sammy are arrested, and Mickey is sent to prison for seven years.

During his time in jail, Mickey suffers from depression, and he's prescribed pills. Mrs Johnstone sings: *"And treats his ills with daily pills / Just like Marilyn Monroe."*

Comment: Marilyn Monroe became addicted to barbiturates, a group of drugs that have a sedative effect. She took an accidental overdose which killed her. Previously, references to Monroe represented happiness, but now Russell uses Monroe to remind the audience about the dangers of abusing prescription pills, which foreshadows Mickey's addiction issues.

Act Two continued

Linda visits Mickey in prison, and tries to encourage him to stop taking the pills, but Mickey refuses. It's clear that Mickey has developed an addiction.

> **Comment:** Russell hints at the building tension in Mickey and Linda's relationship. Mickey is driving Linda away, even though she's trying to support him. This helps to explain why Linda eventually cheats on Mickey.

Mickey gets out of prison early for *"good behaviour"* but he's a changed man: *"he's feelin' fifteen years older / And his speech is rather slow"*.

Linda tells Mrs Johnstone that she's got Mickey a job and a new house, but she's vague about who helped her: *"Oh, just some... some feller I know."*

> **Comment:** The audience suspects that it was Edward who helped with the job and house. Linda's reluctance to admit that Edward was responsible hints that Linda feels guilty about accepting Edward's help.

Despite his new job and new house, Mickey is still addicted to his pills. He tries to come off them, but he experiences withdrawal symptoms of *"shakin' an' sweatin'"*.

Mickey tells Linda he knows that Edward helped with the house and job, and he's angry.

Linda secretly meets Edward, and Mrs Johnstone narrates their meeting during the song *Light Romance*.

> **Comment:** Mrs Johnstone admits there's *"Nothing wrong"* with Edward and Linda's *"light romance"*. This suggests that Mrs Johnstone recognises that Linda feels trapped in her relationship with Mickey, and that Linda deserves to be happy.

Linda and Edward kiss and *"walk together, hand-in-hand"*.

> **Comment:** Linda's affair with Edward gives her freedom from being a housewife, where she's washing a *"million dishes"* and *"always making tea"*. For more on gender, turn to **page 55**.

Mrs Lyons finds Mickey, and points to Edward and Linda holding hands, exposing their affair. In a rage, Mickey goes to his mother's house and retrieves the gun hidden under the floorboards. Mrs Johnstone sees Mickey exit with the gun.

Mickey is described as *"breaking through groups of people, looking, searching, desperate"*. Mrs Johnstone *"frantically"* tries to catch him.

> **Comment:** This frenzied scene increases the tension for the audience. The audience wonders what Mickey will do and if Mrs Johnstone will be able to stop him.

GCSE English Literature | Blood Brothers

Act Two continued

The Narrator comments that the *"devil's got your number / … he's callin' your number up today / Today / Today / TODAY!"*

Comment: The Narrator's ominous lines increase the tension. It's clear that the twins are about to meet their fate.

Mickey enters the Town Hall where Edward is delivering a speech, and aims the gun at Edward. Mickey accuses Edward of having an affair with Linda, suggesting that Edward could be the father of his child: *"You an' Linda were friends when she first got pregnant"*.

Two policemen enter, telling Mickey that a sniper is aiming at him. Mickey admits to Edward: *"I thought I was gonna shoot y'. But I can't even do that."*

Comment: This momentarily de-escalates the tension. The audience hopes that the brothers can resolve their issues.

Mrs Johnstone enters the Town Hall, pleading with Mickey not to shoot Edward. She tells him that Edward is his twin brother and that she gave him away.

Mickey is furious and screams, *"Why didn't you give me away?"*.

Comment: Mickey thinks his life would have been better if he was the twin that was given away.

In his rage, he waves the gun, and it accidentally fires, shooting and killing Edward. The police sniper then shoots Mickey.

Comment: The twins die suddenly which makes their deaths even more shocking.

The Narrator comments: *"And do we blame superstition for what came to pass? / Or could it be what we, the English, have come to know as class?"*

Comment: The Narrator questions whether the twins were destined to die, or whether their deaths could have been prevented if they hadn't been raised in different social classes.

The play ends with Mrs Johnstone speaking her opening lines, *"Tell me it's not true, / Say it's just a story"*.

Comment: This reminds the audience of the play's cyclical structure, and how the Narrator's ominous prologue has come true.

The tragic final scene of the play.

CHARACTERS: MRS JOHNSTONE

Mrs Johnstone is Mickey and Edward's mother. She's a single parent who tries her best but struggles to make ends meet.

Comment: Mrs Johnstone is presented as a realistic character: she's flawed, but she also has a lot of redeemable qualities. Although she makes some poor decisions, she tries to do what's right for her family.

Act One

Haggard: Mrs Johnstone is *"thirty but looks more like fifty"*.

Comment: Mrs Johnstone has had a tough life, and it's taken its toll on her appearance.

Sympathetic: Mrs Johnstone married young after accidentally falling pregnant. Her husband left her for another woman when she was pregnant with her eighth child.

Comment: It's important that the audience sympathises with Mrs Johnstone's situation to understand why she decides to give one of the twins away.

Mrs Johnstone is presented as a sympathetic character.

Poor: As a working-class, single-parent, Mrs Johnstone struggles to feed her children.

Comment: Russell uses Mrs Johnstone to show how people could be trapped by a cycle of poverty. Working-class characters like Mrs Johnstone, Linda and Mickey want a better life, but they have few opportunities to make it happen. This was especially true for women who weren't financially independent and relied on their husbands for money.

Superstitious: Mrs Johnstone is shocked when Mrs Lyons puts her new shoes on the table because she thinks it'll bring bad luck.

Comment: Mrs Lyons exploits Mrs Johnstone's superstitious nature to control her. Mrs Lyons invents the superstition about *"secretly parted"* twins dying if they ever find out they've been separated. This prevents Mrs Johnstone from revealing the truth to her sons.

Desperate: When Mrs Johnstone discovers she's pregnant with twins, she's devastated. She knows she cannot afford to provide for another two children.

Comment: The Narrator calls Mrs Johnstone a *"mother so cruel"* for giving one of the twins away, but her actions could be interpreted as selfless. She wants her son to have a better a life, and she knows that she won't be able to give him what she needs if she keeps him.

GCSE English Literature | Blood Brothers

Mrs Johnstone, Act One continued

Easily manipulated: Mrs Johnstone is easily controlled and influenced by people around her, which means that she makes poor choices:
- Her husband flattered her to get her into bed, telling her she was *"sexier than Marilyn Monroe"*. She fell pregnant and married him. Their relationship didn't last, and he abandoned her, leaving her with eight children.
- Mrs Lyons convinces her to give up one of the twins. This has a devastating impact on her and the rest of characters.
- She orders items from catalogues that she can't afford, which end up getting repossessed.

Comment: Because Mrs Johnstone's life is tough, she's easily persuaded by promises of a better life.

Loving: She is affectionate towards her children. She *"hugs"* Mickey and *"Cradles"* Edward when he's upset about moving house.

Comment: Mrs Johnstone's warmth contrasts with Mrs Lyons' strict attitude.

Act Two

Lonely: Mrs Johnstone goes out dancing with Joe the milkman. It's a reminder that she's more than just a mother; she's also a woman who wants to be happy.

Comment: For more on the theme of gender, turn to **page 55**.

Perceptive: Mrs Johnstone suspects that the twins are going to see *Nymphomaniac Nights* and *Swedish Au Pairs* at the cinema. She doesn't stop them, instead she just calls them *"randy sods"*.

Mrs Johnstone is understanding.

Comment: Mrs Johnstone is more liberal with her children than Mrs Lyons is with Edward. As a result, she has a close relationship with Mickey who says, *"Mam. I love y'"*.

Tolerant: When Mickey tells Mrs Johnstone that he got Linda pregnant, she isn't angry. She says she would be a *"hypocrite"* if she got mad, because she had a pregnancy outside of marriage too.

Comment: Mrs Johnstone's tolerance towards her children isn't always the best thing for them. Her lack of discipline could be partially to blame for Sammy's destructive behaviour.

Devastated: Mrs Johnstone is in disbelief when the twins die. She sings: *"Tell me it's not true, / Say it's just a story"*.

Comment: The audience is left to form their own opinion about whether Mrs Johnstone is to blame for the twins' deaths, or if she's a victim of an unfair class system.

How far does Russell present Mrs Johnstone as irresponsible in *Blood Brothers*?

Write about:
- what Mrs Johnstone says and does
- how far Russell presents Mrs Johnstone as irresponsible.

[30 + 4 marks]

Your answer may include:

AO1 — show understanding of the text
- Mrs Johnstone is financially irresponsible which affects her children. She orders furniture from catalogues that she knows she can't afford, which eventually gets repossessed.
- Mrs Johnstone cannot control her children, and the welfare services threaten to remove them from her care, suggesting that she is an irresponsible parent. Mrs Johnstone's inability to discipline her children could be to blame for Sammy's worsening behaviour, which results in him shooting someone during the robbery.
- Mrs Johnstone's decision to give Edward away could be interpreted as both responsible and irresponsible. Although it seems reckless to give her child to a virtual stranger, Mrs Johnstone gives Edward away so that he can have a better life, and so there is less financial pressure on the rest of her family who are already struggling to get by.
- Despite Mrs Johnstone's tendency to make irresponsible decisions, she is a warm and loving mother, and forms a close bond with both Mickey and Edward. Edward thinks she's "fabulous" and Mickey confides in her when Linda falls pregnant.

AO2 — show understanding of the writer's language choices
- Mrs Johnstone begins the play with a soliloquy describing how her husband left her for another woman when she was pregnant. This helps the audience to understand Mrs Johnstone's difficult situation and creates sympathy for her.
- Mrs Lyons uses forceful language to convince Mrs Johnstone to give Edward away. She uses imperative verbs to make her request seem like a demand, and interrupts Mrs Johnstone so that Mrs Johnstone doesn't have the opportunity to think carefully about her decision.

AO3 — relate the play to the context
- When Mrs Johnstone falls pregnant with her first child, she does the 'responsible' thing and marries Mr Johnstone. She conforms to society's expectations by marrying the father of her child, even though Mr Johnstone ends up treating her poorly.
- Russell uses Mrs Johnstone to suggest that working-class people, especially women, could often get trapped in a cycle of poverty due to their lack of education. Women were especially affected because they were expected to stay at home and raise children, so had fewer opportunities to gain financial independence.

This answer should be marked in accordance with the levels-based mark scheme on page 61.

Make sure your answer to this question is in paragraphs and full sentences. Bullet points have been used in this example answer to suggest some information you could include. There are four marks available for spelling, punctuation and grammar, so make sure you read through your answer carefully, correcting any mistakes.

CHARACTERS: MRS LYONS

Mrs Lyons is a wealthy housewife who employs Mrs Johnstone as a cleaner. She persuades Mrs Johnstone to give her one of her twins. This decision causes Mrs Lyons to become increasingly paranoid.

Act One

Wealthy: Mrs Lyons lives in a big house and doesn't have to work because her husband earns a good salary. She employs Mrs Johnstone to clean her house.

> **Comment:** Mrs Lyons complains about the size of her house: *"It's a pity it's so big"*. She doesn't realise how fortunate she is compared to Mrs Johnstone.

Maternal: Mrs Lyons is desperate to have children, but she isn't able to have children of her own: *"We've been trying for such a long time now"*.

Mrs Lyons puts pressure on Mrs Johnstone to give her one of the twins.

> **Comment:** In the late twentieth century, there was an expectation on married women to have children. Being unable to have a family may have made Mrs Lyons feel inadequate, which creates sympathy for her character. For more on gender roles, turn to **page 55**.

Manipulative: She uses several tactics to persuade Mrs Johnstone to give up one of the twins:
- She uses rhetorical questions to exploit Mrs Johnstone's fears about her children being taken away from her: *"how can you possibly avoid some of them being put into care?"*
- She makes a false promise that Mrs Johnstone can see the baby *"every day"*.
- She uses emotional blackmail to remind Mrs Johnstone that she can't have children of her own, and that she's desperate to be a mother.
- She promises Mrs Johnstone the baby will have a better life, and that he will have access to all the things Mrs Johnstone's children don't, like *"a bed of his own"* and *"all his own toys"*.
- She offers the baby a chance to escape the cycle of poverty that the Johnstones are stuck in: *"He could never be told / To stand and queue up / For hours on end at the dole."*
- As soon as Mrs Johnstone looks like she could be convinced, Mrs Lyons doesn't give Mrs Johnstone time to think. She immediately asks for help with the fake pregnancy.
- She exploits Mrs Johnstone's superstitious nature and pretends that parted twins can never know they are separated, or else they will die. She also makes Mrs Johnstone swear on the Bible, to make a *"binding agreement"*.

> **Comment:** There are hints that Mrs Johnstone is Catholic (she has a picture of the Pope in her house). Mrs Lyons exploits Mrs Johnstone's faith by forcing her to swear on the Bible.

Mrs Lyons, Act One continued

Possessive: Mrs Lyons dislikes Mrs Johnstone paying attention to the baby, so she fires Mrs Johnstone so she's no longer part of Edward's life.

> **Comment:** Mrs Lyons almost immediately goes back on her promise to allow Mrs Johnstone to see the baby *"every day"*. This highlights Mrs Lyons' callous nature: she doesn't care about Mrs Johnstone once she's got what she wanted from her.

Devious: Mrs Lyons makes Mr Lyons believe that Edward is his son. She also lies about her reasons for sacking Mrs Johnstone, by pretending her cleaning has *"deteriorated"* when she just wants to keep Mrs Johnstone and Edward apart.

> **Comment:** Mrs Lyons is prepared to go to extreme lengths to keep Edward and fulfil her desire to be a mother.

Strict: Mrs Lyons hits Edward when he swears.

> **Comment:** Before she has Edward, Mrs Lyons romanticises what motherhood would be like. She thinks she would be a gentle and kind mother: *"I'll pull out his splinters / Without making him cry"*. However, in reality, she struggles to control herself when he misbehaves, suggesting that she finds motherhood challenging.

Prejudiced: Mrs Lyons thinks Mickey and his friends are *"horrible"* who speak *"filth"* and she doesn't want Edward *"mixing with boys like that"*.

> **Comment:** Middle-class people often felt that they were 'better' than working-class people.

Paranoid: Mrs Lyons convinces Mr Lyons to move away from Liverpool because she doesn't want Edward becoming close to the Johnstone family.

> **Comment:** Mrs Lyons' paranoia builds as the play progresses, and her insecurities make her behave irrationally.

Act Two

Volatile: When Mrs Lyons finds out that the Johnstones have moved to Skelmersdale, she's furious. She tracks down Mrs Johnstone, and initially tries to bribe her with *"thousands"* to move away. When that doesn't work, she attacks Mrs Johnstone with a knife.

> **Comment:** The frightening atmosphere created by the attack is reinforced by the children's voices heard off-stage chanting about a *"Mad woman, mad woman living on the hill"*.

Vengeful: Mrs Lyons informs Mickey about Edward and Linda's relationship. It's never explained why Mrs Lyons reveals the affair, so her actions seem spiteful: she betrays Edward and doesn't care if the affair makes him happy.

> **Comment:** Mrs Lyons doesn't have any lines in this scene, instead she just *"points out"* the affair to Mickey. This speeds up the pace of the scene and increases the tension.

CHARACTERS: MR LYONS

Mr Lyons is Mrs Lyons' husband. He has a good job and works long hours to provide for his family. He's the only father figure represented in the play.

Comment: Mr Lyons doesn't appear very often, and when he does, he's often distracted by work. Russell could be suggesting that men often neglected their responsibilities as parents.

Act One

Dedicated to his job: Mr Lyons goes away on business for nine months.

Comment: Mr Lyons is the breadwinner of the family. It was typical in middle-class households for the husband to provide for the family, and for the wife to look after the home. Mr Lyons sees the house as Mrs Lyons' *"domain"*. For more on gender roles, see **page 55**.

Preoccupied: Mr Lyons' commitment to his job means he's often not around to help raise Edward: *"Mummy will read the story, Edward. I've got to go to work for an hour"*.

Comment: Mrs Lyons is concerned about Mr Lyons' lack of involvement with Edward. She's worried that Edward will grow apart from him.

Dismissive: When the baby arrives, Mr Lyons thinks his wife has a *"depression thing"* and when Mrs Lyons is concerned about Edward mixing with 'the wrong crowd', Mr Lyons blames his wife's *"nerves"*. He's quick to dismiss his wife's feelings.

Comment: Men in the late twentieth century tended not to talk about emotions or their feelings. Mr Lyons would rather blame Mrs Lyons' unhappiness on a medical condition than communicate with her to understand why she is unhappy.

Act Two

Uncompassionate: Mr Lyons fires Mickey and the other factory workers during the song *Take a Letter Miss Jones*. He calls the workers *"surplus to requirement"* which suggests he sees them as a disposable workforce, rather than as individuals.

Comment: Since Mr Lyons is from the middle class and probably holds a senior or managerial role at the factory, he isn't affected by the job losses. This reflects how the working classes were the most badly affected by the closure of industry in the late twentieth century.

CHARACTERS: MICKEY JOHNSTONE

Mickey is the twin that Mrs Johnstone keeps. He grows up in a rough part of Liverpool. He can be cheeky and naughty, but he has a sensitive side too.

Act One

Picked on: Mickey's picked on by his elder siblings, especially his older brother, Sammy, who steals his toys.

> **Comment:** Even though Sammy bullies Mickey, Mickey looks up to him. Without a father figure, Sammy is Mickey's only male role model.

Naughty: Mickey's picked up bad behaviour from Sammy. He tries to wee through people's letterboxes, and he knows the 'F' word.

> **Comment:** Although he's naughty sometimes, Mickey still has an innocent side. He's too short to wee through the letterboxes, and he doesn't know what the 'F' word means. This reminds the audience of his youth, and makes him an endearing character.

Russell presents Mickey as a likeable character to make his downfall even more tragic.

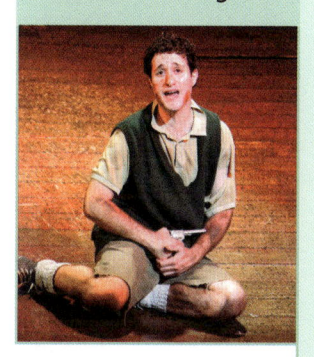

Friendly: Mickey and Edward become best friends when they first meet, even though they have had very different upbringings and don't seem to have much in common.

> **Comment:** Mickey and Edward's instant friendship could be because of their brotherly connection, but it could also be because they're both lonely: Edward is an only child, and Mickey is the youngest child who is picked on by his older siblings.

Sensitive: Mickey is upset when the children tell him he's going to hell for saying the 'F' word.

> **Comment:** Mickey tries to act tough to impress the other children. He pretends that he's been *"caught loads of times by a policeman"*, but when the police officer catches him throwing rocks, he's *"terrified"* and starts crying.

Act Two

> **Comment:** Mickey is 14 at the start of Act Two. Over the course of the act, the audience sees him aged 18, and then in his mid-twenties.

Insecure: At the start of Act Two, Mickey is presented as a typical teenager. He's insecure about how he looks, and he struggles to tell Linda how he feels.

> **Comment:** Edward is also self-conscious about his appearance. Their shared insecurities show how alike they are.

GCSE English Literature | Blood Brothers

Mickey Johnstone, Act Two continued

Loyal: Mickey defends Sammy when he robs the bus, telling the conductor: *"He didn't mean it"*.

Comment: Even though Sammy treats Mickey badly, Mickey still tries to protect him.

Not academic: Because of his background, Mickey struggles at school and finds it *"borin'"*.

Comment: Mickey's limited education means that he has fewer opportunities when he grows up. Access to education is one way that Russell illustrates the class divide between Mickey and Edward. See **page 46** for more.

Hard-working: Mickey gets a job at the box factory and he takes on overtime to earn extra money.

Comment: Unlike Sammy, Mickey gets a job and works extra hours. The audience hopes that Mickey's work ethic might give him a chance to succeed at life.

Unemployed: Mickey is laid off from the factory through no fault of his own. He's desperate to find a job and spends three months looking for work.

Comment: Mickey is presented as a victim of the economic downturn that happened in the 70s and 80s. This presents him as a sympathetic character.

Resentful: When Edward comes home from university, Mickey resents Edward's freedom and lack of responsibilities. Mickey thinks Edward's *"still a kid"*.

Comment: This is a turning point in Mickey and Edward's relationship. Following this scene, Mickey and Edward don't share dialogue until the very end of Act Two. This shows how their different social classes have driven them apart.

Desperate: Mickey agrees to be involved in Sammy's robbery because he's desperate for money.

Comment: Mickey plans to spend his money from the robbery on a meal and new clothes for Linda. This shows his generosity, but like Mrs Johnstone, he's financially irresponsible.

Depressed: Mickey becomes depressed in prison. He's prescribed pills to help treat his depression.

Comment: Mickey becomes dependent on the pills. They make him feel *"invisible"* and change his personality, causing his relationship with Linda to suffer.

Enraged: When he finds out about Edward and Linda's affair, Mickey intends to get revenge by shooting Edward. His depression and addiction have made him mentally unstable.

Comment: Mickey's distraught by the affair because Linda was the only good thing left in his life. When he finds out she's been unfaithful, he hits rock bottom and believes shooting Edward is the only way to make himself feel better.

Mickey realises that he can't pull the trigger. His good morals stop him from shooting Edward. The fact that the gun goes off accidentally makes the final scene even more tragic.

How does Russell use Mickey to comment on society in *Blood Brothers*?

Write about:
- what Mickey says and does
- how Russell uses Mickey to comment on society.

[30 + 4 marks]

Your answer may include:

AO1 — show understanding of the text
- As a working-class character, Mickey is given few opportunities in life. He attends a state school, and his education only prepares him for a job as a factory worker. Russell contrasts Mickey's education with Edward's to show how different the boys' lives are because of class.
- When Mickey is made unemployed, he struggles to find another job, which leads him to participate in the robbery with Sammy. Russell suggests that working-class people could be forced to commit crimes to make ends meet because they had limited options.
- When Mickey finds out that Edward is his twin, he says "Why didn't you give me away?". Mickey believes his working-class upbringing is responsible for his difficult life.

AO2 — show understanding of the writer's language choices
- Mickey's dialogue presents him as a working-class character. Russell uses phonetic spellings, apostrophes and dialect words to show his speech patterns.
- Russell juxtaposes the scenes showing how the police officer responds to Mickey and Edward throwing stones. The police officer blames Mickey, highlighting how society was often prejudiced towards the working class.
- Russell structures the play so the audience watches Mickey grow up from aged 8 to his mid-twenties. This allows the audience to see first-hand the difficulties that Mickey has had to overcome throughout his life.

AO3 — relate the play to the context
- Blood Brothers is an example of a tragedy, and Russell hints that Mickey's working-class background is his fatal flaw which is ultimately responsible for his downfall.
- Russell uses Mickey to show how working-class people could get trapped in a cycle of poverty because they were denied access to education and opportunities through lack of money. Russell suggests that the class system is unfair.
- When Mickey is fired from the factory, it's through no fault of his own. He's shown to be a hard-working employee who takes on overtime. Because of this, Mickey is shown to be a victim of the economic downturn in Liverpool in the 80s.

This answer should be marked in accordance with the levels-based mark scheme on page 61.

⭐ Make sure your answer to this question is in paragraphs and full sentences. Bullet points have been used in this example answer to suggest some information you could include. There are four marks available for spelling, punctuation and grammar, so make sure you read through your answer carefully, correcting any mistakes.

CHARACTERS: EDWARD LYONS

Edward is the twin who is taken by Mrs Lyons. He's brought up in a middle-class family and has access to opportunities that Mickey doesn't. This eventually causes Mickey to resent Edward and drives the twins apart.

Act One

Comment: Edward is seven for most of Act One.

Naïve: Edward is trusting and innocent compared to the more street-wise Mickey. He shares his sweets freely and is impressed by Mickey's swearing and naughty behaviour.

Comment: Edward has had a more privileged upbringing. As an only child from a middle-class family, he's never wanted for anything so he's generous with his sweets. This contrasts with the Johnstone children who have less to go around, so they steal each other's toys.

Well-mannered: Edward is polite, calling Mickey's mum *"Mrs Johnstone"*.

Comment: Even from a young age, there's a big difference between how the boys speak, behave and dress. Edwards speaks in standard English (see **page 12**) whereas Mickey has a regional accent. Edward is polite and well-behaved, whereas Mickey is cheeky and rude. Costume departments may dress Edward in smart clothing, whereas Mickey's clothes might be dirty, poorly fitting and full of holes.

Rebellious: Edward sneaks out of his house to play with Mickey and Linda, even though his mother has forbidden it.

Comment: Edward's attracted to the excitement and freedom of spending time with Mickey and Linda. He's got a wild, rebellious streak, just like Mickey.

Eager to impress: Edward agrees to throw stones at the windows to impress Mickey and Linda.

Comment: Occasionally, Edward adopts a more regional accent to fit in with Mickey and Linda. In Act Two, Edward says: *"She's off her beam, my ma"*.

Edward is smothered by Mrs Lyons. She's strict and overly protective, partly because she doesn't want him to cross paths with the Johnstones. Ironically, Mrs Lyons' overbearing nature encourages Edward to seek out Mickey, and form a close relationship with Mrs Johnstone who gives him the affection he craves.

Although Mrs Lyons provides Edward with a nice house, and plenty of food and toys, Edward is still drawn to the Johnstone family. Russell could be suggesting that material possessions aren't a substitute for a warm, loving family.

Edward wears smart clothes that are neat and tidy.

Act Two

Comment: Edward is 14 at the start of Act Two. Over the course of the act, we see him aged 18, and then in his mid-twenties.

Academic: Edward is *"doing very well"* at school, and there's *"Talk of Oxbridge"* (Oxford and Cambridge Universities, the two most prestigious universities in the UK).

Comment: Edward is privately educated, and this has allowed him to excel academically. Russell could be suggesting that if Mickey had the same opportunities as Edward, he could have also been academically gifted.

Edward's middle-class upbringing means he has more opportunities than Mickey.

Loyal: Edward encourages Mickey to ask Linda out, even though Edward also has feelings for her: *"stare straight into her eyes, and you say 'Linda, I love you"*.

Comment: Edward says charming women is *"easy"* because he's *"read about it"*. A lot of Edward's knowledge comes from books, rather than real-world experience. This contrasts with the street-wise Mickey and hints that Edward can sometimes be out-of-touch with reality.

Immature: When Mickey loses his job, Edward insensitively tells Mickey, *"sod it and draw the dole"*. He doesn't understand how difficult it is to be unemployed.

Comment: Edward's never had to worry about finances, so he struggles to empathise with Mickey's situation. When Edward tells Mickey he has *"plenty"* of money, Mickey refuses to accept Edward's money. This reminds the audience how Mrs Lyons tried to bribe Mrs Johnstone to move away from Skelmersdale. Russell suggests that middle-class people sometimes attempted to use money to solve their problems.

After Edward comes home from university, he doesn't have much dialogue, and his affair with Linda is only shown visually. This allows Russell to focus the audience's attention on Mickey's downward spiral which is the main source of tension.

Successful: When Edward is in his mid-twenties, he's a local councillor. He has enough power and influence in the local community to get Mickey a job and a house.

Comment: Russell contrasts Edward's successful life with Mickey's difficulties. Russell shows the impact that money and the class system can have on a person's life. For more on the theme of class, turn to **page 46**.

Deceitful: After years of suppressing their feelings for each other, Edward and Linda start an affair.

Comment: Although Edward and Linda betray Mickey, their affair is presented sympathetically because Mickey has pushed both of them away.

CHARACTERS: LINDA

Linda is a childhood friend of Mickey and Edward. She falls in love with Mickey, and they get married, but her affair with Edward leads to the twins' downfall.

Act One

Brave: Linda defends Mickey when the other children tell him he's *"gonna die"* for saying the 'F' word. She stands up to Sammy, who is several years older than her, and threatens to tell her mother that Sammy's stolen her cigarettes and *"half-crowns"*.

Comment: Linda subverts gender stereotypes by defending a boy. For more on gender, turn to **page 55**.

Act Two

Vocal: She's open about her feelings for Mickey, and isn't embarrassed to tell Mickey that she loves him.

Comment: Even though Linda makes her feelings towards Mickey clear, she waits for him to ask her out. She conforms to gender stereotypes by expecting Mickey to take the lead in their relationship.

Linda is presented as a sympathetic character.

Housewife: Linda quickly falls pregnant after starting a relationship with Mickey. They get married when they're only 18.

Comment: Like Mrs Johnstone, Linda seems destined to fulfil the role of mother and housewife. Russell suggests that despite being strong willed, Linda is doomed to become trapped in the cycle of working-class poverty.

Supportive: Linda stands by Mickey when he goes to prison, and she encourages him to give up the anti-depressants. She helps Mickey get a new job, and finds them a house to live in.

Comment: Despite her loyalty to Mickey, and her attempts to improve their lives, Mickey's depression and drug addiction puts a strain on their relationship.

Unhappy: Linda admits that she gets *"depressed"* and feels bored and trapped by her life as a housewife washing a *"million dishes"* and *"always making tea"*.

Comment: This creates sympathy for Linda. Her desire for excitement and freedom from her responsibilities helps to explain why she has an affair with Edward.

Unfaithful: Linda has a *"light romance"* with Edward.

Comment: There are hints that Edward and Linda have feelings for each other throughout Act Two. This makes their affair seem more believable and genuine.

CHARACTERS: SAMMY JOHNSTONE

Sammy is Mrs Johnstone's son and Mickey's older brother. He's an unpleasant bully, whose behaviour starts as naughty and escalates to criminal.

> **Comment:** As a child, Mickey is both afraid of Sammy and idolises him. Without a father, Sammy is Mickey's only male role-model. This complicated relationship helps to explain why Mickey agrees to be Sammy's lookout during the robbery.

Act One

Naughty: Sammy steals Mickey's toys, he *"wees"* through letterboxes and plays with matches.

> **Comment:** Sammy's a bad influence on his younger brother: Mickey copies Sammy's naughty behaviour.

Bully: Sammy joins in when the other children bully Mickey for saying the 'F' word. Sammy doesn't try to defend or protect his younger brother, even when he's upset.

> **Comment:** Mickey is constantly in Sammy's shadow as a child. When Mickey befriends Edward, Mickey finally has an opportunity to be the confident and assertive leader.

Act Two

Badly behaved: Sammy's behaviour worsens. He burns down his school in Skelmersdale.

> **Comment:** Mrs Johnstone says *"it's easily done"* showing that she doesn't take responsibility for Sammy's bad behaviour. Mrs Johnstone's lack of discipline could be partly to blame for Sammy's escalating violence.

Sammy represents negative working-class stereotypes.

Violent: He tries to rob the bus conductor at knifepoint.

> **Comment:** The robbery wasn't planned: Sammy only threatens the bus conductor because he wouldn't let him have a cheaper bus fare. This suggests that Sammy is quick to anger, and he doesn't think about the consequences of his actions. This foreshadows Sammy shooting the man during the filling station robbery.

Lazy: Sammy is on the dole, but unlike Mickey, he makes no effort to find a job.

> **Comment:** Sammy conforms to negative working-class stereotypes.

Influential: Sammy persuades Mickey to take part in the filling station robbery.

> **Comment:** Sammy uses rhetorical questions to humiliate Mickey and convince him to take part in the robbery: *"Where y' takin' y' tart for New Year? Nowhere."*

GCSE English Literature | Blood Brothers

CHARACTERS: THE NARRATOR

The Narrator is an ominous presence throughout the play. Every time he appears on stage, he reminds the audience of the twins' fate. He occasionally interacts with the main characters when he plays a few minor roles.

Acts One and Two

Comment: Unlike the other characters, the Narrator doesn't seem to develop, age or change. The fact that he's unaffected by time or the events of the play adds to his mysterious and omniscient character.

Heartless: The Narrator introduces Mrs Johnstone as a *"mother so cruel"* and encourages the audience to judge her.

Comment: The Narrator's lack of sympathy towards Mrs Johnstone could reflect how working-class people often face prejudice.

All-knowing: The Narrator delivers the prologue, telling the audience about the downfall of the Johnstone twins. His knowledge of future events makes him seem powerful.

Comment: The Narrator's ominous prologue is reinforced by his use of rhyme and old-fashioned language (*"Of one womb born"*). This creates a sinister atmosphere.

Unnerving: The Narrator often reminds the audience about the theme of superstition. He references images associated with bad luck such as *"shoes upon the table an' a joker in the pack"*.

Comment: The Narrator's comments often create an unsettling mood, reminding the audience that the twins are doomed. For more on the theme of fate and superstition, turn to **page 52**.

The Narrator helps create an unsettling atmosphere throughout the play.

Russell also uses the Narrator as a structural device. He links some scenes, and indicates a change of time or setting to the audience. For example, he narrates the montage in Act Two when the twins and Linda age from 14 to 18, and helps the audience understand how much time has passed.

The Narrator also reminds the audience that the play is a tragedy and that any moments of happiness will be short-lived.

Other characters

The Narrator also appears as several minor characters. These characters often deliver bad news or create conflict, allowing the Narrator to influence the actions of the main characters.

Comment: When he's playing the role of the Narrator, he cannot be seen or heard by the other characters. However, when he becomes one of the several minor characters, he can interact with the other characters.

Act One

Milkman: As the milkman, he demands that Mrs Johnstone pays her milk bill, and has no sympathy when Mrs Johnstone tells him that she's pregnant and needs milk.

Gynaecologist: He tells Mrs Johnstone that she's expecting twins and has two more *"Mouths to feed"*. This reinforces Mrs Johnstone's concerns about not being able to provide for an additional child.

Act Two

Bus conductor: As the bus conductor, he threatens Mrs Johnstone by saying *"No one gets off without the price bein' paid"*, reminding her that she owes a debt for giving Edward away.

Edward's teacher: He speaks aggressively to Edward, saying *"Getting rather big for your boots, aren't you?"*. He demands to see Edward's locket and suspends him from school. Edward's suspension causes Mrs Lyons to find out about the locket, and spy on her son.

Mickey's teacher: He tries to humiliate Mickey when he can't answer his question, and the teacher suspends Mickey and Linda when they are cheeky.

Comment: Because the Narrator plays several different roles throughout the play, the audience is never sure of his true identity, especially since some of his characters have working-class professions (the milkman) and some have middle-class professions (the gynaecologist). This reinforces his mysterious and omniscient nature.

GCSE English Literature | Blood Brothers

THEMES: SOCIAL CLASS

Russell demonstrates how people can have very different opportunities depending on the social class they were raised in.

Social class

The Lyonses are presented as a typical middle-class family, whereas the Johnstones are a typical working-class family. Even though the families live close to each other in Liverpool and Skelmersdale, their lives are very different.

Money

The Lyons family: Middle-class families were financially comfortable and could afford everything they needed. Mr Lyons gives his wife *"fifty pounds"* without really questioning it.

The Johnstone family: Working-class families often didn't have much money and struggled to get by. Mrs Johnstone can't afford to feed her children properly and her milk bill is overdue.

Jobs

The Lyons family: Middle-class people often had well-paid, skilled jobs, which often required a good education. Mr Lyons is a manager at a factory and Edward becomes a *"Councillor"*. Well-paid jobs often gave people power in the local community, for example, Edward is able to arrange a job and a house for Mickey.

The Johnstone family: Working-class families had low-paid, unskilled jobs that required little to no education. Mickey works in a cardboard box factory in a job he *"hated"*.

Women

The Lyons family: Middle-class wives often didn't need to work because their husbands could support them financially. Mrs Lyons doesn't have a job, and she can afford to employ Mrs Johnstone to clean her house.

The Johnstone family: Working-class women were expected to get jobs to contribute to the family's income. Mrs Johnstone has a job as a cleaner and her wage supports her whole family.

Secondary Education

The Lyons family: Middle-class families could afford to send their children to private schools if they didn't pass the grammar school entrance exam. These schools offered children a good education and connections which could help them get well-paid jobs as adults. Edward attends a private all-boys school where he does well academically.

The Johnstone family: Working-class children went to the local free state school. Mickey and Linda find school *"borin'"*. The teacher calls a pupil a *"turd"* which highlights how there is little respect between teachers and pupils in the play.

Housing

The Lyons family: Middle-class families lived in larger homes in 'nicer' neighbourhoods with access to green spaces. The Lyons live in a large house near a park.

The Johnstone family: Working-class families lived in small, terraced houses in built-up areas. Mickey and his siblings play in the street.

Act Two continued

🎓 Higher Education

The Lyons family: Middle-class children might be expected to go to university. University educations were expensive, so they were only accessible to those who could afford them. Edward goes to university, which allows him to get a good job after he graduates.

The Johnstone family: Working-class children often didn't attend university because they couldn't afford it, and needed to start earning money as soon as they left school. Neither Mickey nor Linda attend university.

💬 Accent

The Lyons family: Middle-class families often speak in standard English with a received pronunciation accent. Edward sounds *"posh"*.

The Johnstone family: Working-class families often speak with regional accents. The Johnstones and Linda speak with a Liverpudlian accent.

🔍 Perception

The Lyons family: Middle-class families had a reputation of being polite and respectable. When the children get in trouble for throwing stones, the policeman treats the Lyons family with respect.

The Johnstone family: Working-class families had a reputation of being rough. Mrs Lyons thinks that Mickey is a *"horrible little boy"* who speaks *"filth"*.

Russell's messages

Attitudes of the middle class

The Lyonses are presented as being indifferent or ignorant to the struggles of the working class.

- Mrs Lyons doesn't sympathise with Mrs Johnstone when she's concerned about having twins. Instead, Mrs Lyons exploits Mrs Johnstone's financial worries for her own benefit.
- Mrs Lyons fires Mrs Johnstone when it suits her, even though she knows Mrs Johnstone needs the money to provide for her family.
- Mr Lyons is unsympathetic when the workers at his factory are laid off. He views them as disposable and simply says it's *"a sign of the times"*.
- Edward doesn't understand why Mickey is so depressed after he loses his job and can't find work. Edward insensitively says, *"So you're not working. Why is it so important?"*.

Money and happiness

Even though Mrs Lyons is well-off, she never seems happy. She spends most of the play paranoid that Mrs Johnstone will take Edward away from her. Mrs Lyons tries to bribe Mrs Johnstone twice: once (successfully) when she fires Mrs Johnstone, and once (unsuccessfully) when she offers to pay Mrs Johnstone to move away from Skelmersdale. Russell could be suggesting that money can't solve all your problems and it can't buy happiness.

Money and society

Russell could be suggesting that British society was unfair. He implies that those born into the working class were often at a disadvantage compared to those born into the upper and middle classes, because they had a harder life, fewer opportunities and little help from their social superiors. This meant that it was difficult for working-class people to escape the cycle of poverty.

GCSE English Literature | Blood Brothers

How does Russell present the importance of social class in *Blood Brothers*?

Write about:
- the importance of social class to characters in the play
- how Russell presents the importance of social class.

[30 + 4 marks]

Your answer may include:

AO1 — show understanding of the text
- Social class is the predominant theme in Blood Brothers. At the end of the play, the Narrator suggests that social class could be to blame for the twins' downfall.
- Throughout the play, Russell shows how the boys are given very different opportunities in life because of the class they are raised in. For example, Mickey belongs to the working class, his family are poor, and can barely afford to pay for food. He attends a state school, where his education only prepares him for manual labour. On the other hand, Edward is raised as an only child in a middle-class family. He attends a fee-paying all-boys school, which enables him to go university, which prepares him for a professional job as a councillor. As adults, Mickey struggles to get by while Edward has "plenty" of money.
- Russell also shows how working-class people face prejudice. When the police officer catches the twins throwing stones, he threatens Mrs Johnstone with "the courts". However, when he speaks to the Lyonses, the police officer is more respectful and suggests that it was only a "prank". This shows how working-class families could be treated more harshly by society.

AO2 — show understanding of the writer's language choices
- Russell uses language to highlight the class differences between the working-class Johnstone family and the middle-class Lyons family. The Johnstones speak in a regional accent, which is shown through dialect words and phonetic spellings. However, the Lyons speak in standard English and use language typical of that class, such as "mummy", "smashing" and "super".
- Russell juxtaposes certain scenes to encourage his audience to compare the experiences of the different classes. For example, Russell contrasts Edward's experiences at his private school with Mickey's experiences at his state school. Edward's teacher thinks he's on track to go to Oxbridge, while Mickey's teacher thinks he'll struggle to get a job.

AO3 — relate the play to the context
- Social class is ultimately linked to money. Russell shows that money enables the Lyonses to pay for Edward's education which gives him an advantage as an adult.
- Russell suggests that working-class people could struggle to escape the cycle of poverty because they had limited access to education or money.
- Russell also presents the middle classes as indifferent and ignorant towards the problems faced by the working classes, instead viewing them as disposable. Mr Lyons fires Mickey from the factory, and Mrs Lyons fires Mrs Johnstone from her job as a cleaner, even though Mrs Lyons knows that Mrs Johnstone desperately needs the money.

This answer should be marked in accordance with the levels-based mark scheme on page 61.

> Make sure your answer to this question is in paragraphs and full sentences. Bullet points have been used in this example answer to suggest some information you could include. There are four marks available for spelling, punctuation and grammar, so make sure you read through your answer carefully, correcting any mistakes.

THEMES: FRIENDSHIP

As children, Mickey and Edward form a close friendship. However, as they grow up, the twins' differences eventually cause envy and resentment.

Friendship

Mickey and Edward become best friends from the moment they meet. This could be interpreted as childish naivety, or symbolic of the close connection the boys have as twins.

As children, the boys admire each other's differences:
- Mickey is possessive of his toys because he has to share them with his numerous siblings. Edward, on the other hand, is an only child so he's happy to share his sweets with Mickey. Mickey is impressed by Edward's generosity.
- Mickey admires Edward's vocabulary, and that he knows words like "*dictionary*". Edward is impressed by Mickey's knowledge of swear words.
- Edward is impressed by Mickey's daring behaviour, like shooting the airgun and throwing stones. Mickey offers Edward an escape from his strict and repressed upbringing.

Comment: Despite the twins' different social backgrounds, they become very close. Russell could be suggesting that their bond as twins allows them to overcome their differences, but it could also be because children are less aware of social class than adults, so they are less likely to judge one another. It's only when they're older that they realise how different their lives are.

Envy and resentment

Mickey and Edward are sometimes envious of each other. At the end of Act One, their envy is limited to childish things: Mickey wishes he could be *"clean, neat and tidy"* like Edward, whereas Edward wishes he could *"Kick a ball and climb a tree"* like Mickey.

However, as they grow up, there are stronger hints at the resentment that will drive them apart. When they are 18, Edward is envious of Linda and Mickey's feelings towards each other. He tells Linda: *"If I was Mickey I would have asked you [to marry me] years ago"*.

When Edward gives Mickey a job and a house in Act Two, Mickey is resentful of the power and influence that Edward has over his life: *"It used to be just sweets an' ciggies he gave me... Now it's a job and a house"*.

Comment: Mickey eventually resents the generosity he used to admire in Edward because it reminds him of his own failures.

GCSE English Literature | Blood Brothers

THEMES: GROWING UP

The audience watches the twins grow up into young men. By the time they reach 18, it's clear that Mickey has had to grow up faster than Edward.

Age seven

When the twins are seven, they are presented as typical children.

Comment: Russell makes the twins' language immature and childish to emphasise their youth. For more information, turn to **page 12**.

- Mickey's childhood is quite tough. There are hints that he doesn't always have enough to eat, and what few toys he has are often stolen or broken by his siblings.
- Mickey is frustrated he's *"only seven"* and wishes he was older: *"I wish I was our Sammy / Our Sammy's nearly ten"*.

Comment: Mickey's desire to be older is ironic. When he's eighteen, Mickey wishes he could be a child again so he could be free from his adult responsibilities.

- Mickey's childhood games don't have consequences: if a child 'dies', they just count from one to ten to *"get up off the ground again"*.

Comment: This foreshadows the twins dying at the end of the play. Unlike during the childhood games, Mickey and Edward can't get up off the ground again.

Edward

- Edward's childhood is more privileged than Mickey's. He's happy to share because he always has plenty of toys and sweets.
- Edward's upbringing is more sheltered than Mickey's. Mrs Lyons has protected him from anything inappropriate, such as swearing.

Age fourteen

Even though they lose touch when they move away from Liverpool, the boys rekindle their friendship when they are 14. They are presented as typical teenagers:
- They both get in trouble at school and are suspended.
- They are self-conscious about how they look.

Comment: When the boys meet again in Act Two, they are envious of each other's appearance: *"Each part of his face / Is in just the right place"*. This is ironic, as they are twins.

- Mickey is awkward around girls and finds it difficult to tell Linda how he feels about her.
- The twins are interested in sex and go to see pornographic films at the cinema.

Age eighteen

In the UK, turning 18 is seen as reaching adulthood. It's the age that people can vote, legally buy alcohol, and get married without parental consent.

From age 18, there is a shift in the twins' friendship. Mickey matures faster than Edward due to his responsibilities, and Mickey comes to resent Edward's carefree attitude.

Comment: Russell suggests that 'growing up' isn't just about getting older, it's also about having responsibilities and obligations.

Mickey

- Mickey and Linda fall pregnant, and they get married soon after. Mickey becomes a father with responsibilities: he needs to support his wife and child.
- When Mickey loses his job, he becomes depressed. He tells Edward: *"while no one was looking I grew up"*.

Comment: Mickey is demoralised because no one will employ him, and as the breadwinner, he feels inadequate because he cannot provide for his family.

Mickey and Linda marry when they are 18.

Edward

- While at university, Edward goes to parties and meets *"tremendous"* people. Unlike Mickey, he enjoys his youth and doesn't have any responsibilities or people who depend on him.
- When Mickey tells Edward about being unemployed, Edward doesn't understand the difficulties Mickey faces, telling him, *"draw the dole, live like a bohemian"*.

Comment: Unlike Mickey, Edward has never experienced financial worries. Mickey is frustrated that Edward doesn't understand his situation, telling him: *"you're still a kid"*. Their lives have become so different that they drift apart.

Aged mid-twenties

By their mid-twenties, the twins' lives are very different, and they no longer speak to each other.

Mickey

Mickey has spent several years in prison. This contributes to his worsening mental health, and his eventual dependency on his medication.

Comment: After he leaves prison, Mickey is described as looking *"fifteen years older"*. This is similar to Mrs Johnstone being *"aged thirty but looks more like fifty"*, and hints how working-class people seem to age more quickly because of their hardships.

Edward

Edward has a successful job as a local councillor. He doesn't have a wife or children.

GCSE English Literature | Blood Brothers

THEMES: FATE AND SUPERSTITION

Fate is the idea that events are predetermined and destined to happen. Superstitions are actions that are thought to bring good or bad luck.

The Narrator

The Narrator gives away the tragic ending at the very start of the play. This emphasises the inevitability of fate, and how the twins cannot escape their destinies.

The Narrator sings *Shoes Upon the Table*, which reminds the audience of the twins' fate by referencing superstitions associated with bad luck (i.e. a cracked mirror, spilled salt and walking on pavement cracks). These negative images build tension and create an ominous atmosphere.

At the end of the play, the Narrator asks: *"Do we blame superstition for what came to pass?"*

Comment: Russell encourages the audience to make up their own minds about whether superstition is to blame for the twins' death. However, it could be argued that the superstitions themselves aren't powerful, instead it's people's belief in superstitions which makes them vulnerable to being exploited.

Superstition

Mrs Johnstone

Mrs Johnstone is introduced as a superstitious character: she becomes agitated when Mrs Lyons leaves shoes on the table (a sign of bad luck).

Comment: Mrs Johnstone may be superstitious because, as a powerless, working-class woman, believing in superstitions may help give her a sense of control over her life.

Mrs Lyons recognises that she can control Mrs Johnstone by exploiting her superstitious nature. Mrs Lyons makes up a superstition about parted twins dying if they ever find out they are separated. This prevents Mrs Johnstone from ever telling her sons that they are twins.

Mrs Johnstone is a superstitious character.

Superstition continued

Mrs Lyons

Mrs Lyons doesn't believe in superstitions initially and laughs when Mrs Johnstone thinks it's bad luck to put shoes on the table. However, she quickly recognises that she can use superstitions to control Mrs Johnstone, and invents the superstition about separated twins.

As her paranoia grows, Mrs Lyons becomes superstitious and *"sweeps"* the shoes off the table. Mrs Lyons' belief in superstitions is closely linked to her worsening mental health.

Comment: Mrs Lyons is so paranoid about Edward discovering the truth she starts believing in superstitions to try to ward off bad luck. It's ironic that Mrs Lyons initially used superstitions to try to control Mrs Johnstone, but she ends up being controlled by them.

Fate

Mickey and Edward

Although their mothers try to keep them apart, Mickey and Edward's paths keep crossing, which suggests that the twins are fated to be in each other's lives:

- Mickey's mother tells him not to play near the *"big houses in the park"* because that's where Edward lives. Edward's mother tells him not to play near Mickey's house too. Both children ignore their mothers, and the boys meet.

- The Lyonses move to Skelmersdale to escape the Johnstones. Fate causes the Johnstones to move to Skelmersdale too.

- Mickey sometimes sees Edward *"lookin' out the window"*, and the two re-connect after seven years apart. It seems as though their paths were destined to cross again.

Freewill

The opposite of fate is freewill: the idea that people have the power to control their own destiny. Russell shows how each of the characters makes decisions which contribute to the twins' deaths:

These are just some of the decisions that influence the events of the play. There are several more.

- Mrs Lyons suggests separating the twins.
- Mrs Johnstone agrees to give Edward away.
- Mr Lyons fires Mickey from the factory.
- Sammy suggests the robbery.
- Mickey agrees to take part in the robbery.
- Edward and Linda decide to start an affair.
- Mrs Lyons tells Mickey about the affair.

Comment: It could be argued that if just one of the characters had made a different decision, the twins' fate could have been avoided. This is a key element of the tragedy genre: the belief that the tragic ending could have been prevented.

GCSE English Literature | Blood Brothers

How does Russell present the importance of fate and superstition in *Blood Brothers*?

Write about:
- the importance of fate and superstition to characters in the play
- how Russell presents the importance of fate and superstition.

[30 + 4 marks]

Your answer may include:

AO1 — show understanding of the text
- Mrs Johnstone is presented as a superstitious character: she is agitated when Mrs Lyons puts her shoes on the table. Mrs Lyons exploits this by inventing a superstition about parted twins dying if they ever discover the truth. This ensures Mrs Johnstone's silence.
- Initially, Mrs Lyons doesn't believe in superstitions. However, as her mental health deteriorates, she begins to believe in superstitions and "sweeps" shoes off the table. This reinforces Mrs Lyons' desperation to ward off bad luck, and prevent anyone from finding out the truth about Edward. This is ironic, as Mrs Lyons initially used superstitions to control Mrs Lyons, but now they are starting to control her.

AO2 — show understanding of the writer's language choices
- Russell uses a cyclical structure. This suggests that the events of the play are inevitable, and the twins were fated to die. This is also reinforced by the Narrator's prologue, which reveals the ending to the audience and suggests the twins' deaths are inescapable.
- The Narrator sings Shoes Upon the Table and the lyrics reference superstitions associated with bad luck, including spilled salt and cracked mirrors. This creates an ominous atmosphere and reminds the audience that the twins are cursed to die.
- Russell suggests that the twins are destined to be in each other's lives. Even though Mrs Johnstone and Mrs Lyons try their best to keep the boys apart, their paths keep crossing. This implies that fate keeps bringing them together.
- At the end of the play, the Narrator asks whether superstition can be blamed for the twins' deaths. This encourages the audience to reflect on the events of the play, and question their own belief in fate and superstition.

AO3 — relate the play to the context
- Russell suggests that Mrs Johnstone's superstitious beliefs allow her to feel as though she has some control over the events in her life.
- Russell suggests that it is not the superstitions that are powerful, but people's belief in them. Mrs Johnstone's belief in superstitions means that Mrs Lyons can control her.

This answer should be marked in accordance with the levels-based mark scheme on page 61.

> ⭐ Make sure your answer to this question is in paragraphs and full sentences. Bullet points have been used in this example answer to suggest some information you could include. There are four marks available for spelling, punctuation and grammar, so make sure you read through your answer carefully, correcting any mistakes.

THEMES: GENDER

Russell shows that it's not only social class that impacts your life. A person's gender also dictates their experiences.

Gender stereotypes

Women

Women in the late twentieth century were:
- expected to get married young, raise children and look after the house.
- not expected to have a job, but if they did, they earned less than men and held junior roles. For example, Miss Jones is Mr Lyons' assistant.
- expected to be the 'weaker' sex and subservient to men.

Men

Men in the late twentieth century were:
- expected to get married, have children and provide financially for their family.
- expected to be the head of the household, and make decisions on behalf of the family.
- expected to maintain a 'stiff upper lip' and show little emotion.

The women

The female characters in *Blood Brothers* subvert and conform to gender stereotypes.

Mrs Johnstone

Conforms: She gets married young and has a large family. Having children traps Mrs Johnstone in the role of caregiver, and she is expected to raise the children when her husband leaves her.

Subverts: She is the head of the Johnstone family and the sole breadwinner. She raises a large family by herself with no help and little money. She is strong and resilient.

Comment: When her husband leaves her, Mrs Johnstone has to fulfil the role of both father and mother.

Mrs Lyons

Conforms: She is desperate to have children and feels as though she has failed as a woman because she can't have her own. She is a housewife and is the primary caregiver to Edward.

Subverts: She manipulates and deceives her husband by lying to him about Edward.

GCSE English Literature | Blood Brothers

The women, continued

Linda

Conforms: As a teenager, she waits for Mickey to ask her out. She gets pregnant and marries young. At 18, she becomes a housewife responsible for domestic duties, rather than earning a wage. She is financially dependant on men. Mickey is the breadwinner of the family, and when he cannot provide for their family, she turns to Edward for help.

> **Comment:** Russell draws parallels between Mrs Johnstone and Linda. It seems Linda's life will be very similar to Mrs Johnstone's.

Subverts: She stands up to the other children and her teacher to protect Mickey. She is vocal about her feelings for Mickey. As a child and teenager, she's 'one of the boys': she has male friends, shoots the air rifle, and gets into trouble with the police. When she marries Mickey, she tries to make decisions on behalf of the family and gets Mickey a job and house.

Linda is vocal about her feelings for Mickey, but she waits for him to ask her out.

The men

Fathers do not feature as prominently as mothers in *Blood Brothers*.

> **Comment:** Russell mainly focuses on the impact that mothers have on their children.

Mr Lyons

Mr Lyons conforms to male stereotypes. He is the breadwinner and provides financially for his wife and child. He is often at work, so doesn't spend much time bonding with Edward.

He makes decisions on behalf of the family, for example, he doesn't want to adopt, and he decides that they should move to Skelmersdale. Mr Lyons is reluctant to talk about his wife's feelings, instead blaming her *"nerves"*.

Mr Johnstone

Mr Johnstone never appears on stage, but he is presented negatively. He criticises Mrs Johnstone for being *"twice the size of Marilyn Monroe"*, and he abandons her for another woman when she's pregnant. He expects Mrs Johnstone to raise their eight children alone, and he doesn't appear to financially support them.

56   Clear**Revise**

How far does Russell present Linda as a strong female character in *Blood Brothers*?

Write about:
- What Linda says and does
- How far Russell presents Linda as a strong female character.

[30 + 4 marks]

Your answer may include:

AO1 — show understanding of the text
- Linda stands up to the other children when they bully Mickey. She defends Mickey when their teacher attempts to humiliate him. She's strong and defiant and not afraid to get into trouble to protect the people she loves.
- She's very vocal about her feelings for Mickey, telling him that she loves him in front of everyone in the school. She isn't afraid of what people think about her.
- She's proactive and finds a Mickey a job and a house to try to improve their situation. She's self-sufficient and doesn't solely rely on Mickey to provide for their family.
- However, she also conforms to some gender stereotypes. Although she isn't ashamed to admit her love for Mickey, she waits for him to ask her out, showing that she adheres to social conventions where the male takes charge of the relationship.
- When she eventually starts a relationship with Mickey, she quickly falls pregnant and marries Mickey because that is what is expected of her. This traps her in a cycle of poverty, where she is a bored housewife who is stuck "making tea".

AO2 — show understanding of the writer's language choices
- Russell shows Linda's protective nature throughout the play, from childhood all the way up to adulthood. This consistency reinforces her as a positive influence on Mickey.
- Her language can be forceful and direct. She tells Mickey "you've got to start makin' an effort." She isn't afraid to speak her mind.
- Russell draws parallels between Linda and Mrs Johnstone. They both get married young because they fell pregnant, and they both become housewives who struggle to get by. Russell uses this to show how working-class women like Linda have few opportunities in life.

AO3 — relate the play to the context
- Russell uses Linda to show how working-class women could get trapped in a cycle of poverty. Without money and the opportunity to have a good education, Linda is destined to become a housewife and mother who is financially dependant on the men around her.
- Expectations of female behaviour at the time affect Linda's decisions. She's expected to get married when she falls pregnant, becoming a mother when she's only 18.

This answer should be marked in accordance with the levels-based mark scheme on page 61.

> Make sure your answer to this question is in paragraphs and full sentences. Bullet points have been used in this example answer to suggest some information you could include. There are four marks available for spelling, punctuation and grammar, so make sure you read through your answer carefully, correcting any mistakes.

EXAMINATION PRACTICE

1. How does Russell use Mickey to explore the theme of growing up in *Blood Brothers*?

   Write about:
   - what Mickey says and does
   - how Russell presents Mickey in the play as a whole.

   [30 + 4 marks]

2. How does Russell present Mrs Lyons as an important character in the play *Blood Brothers*?

   Write about:
   - what Mrs Lyons says and does
   - how Russell presents Mrs Lyons as an important character in the play.

   [30 + 4 marks]

3. How does Russell use the character of Edward to explore the importance of education in *Blood Brothers*?

   Write about:
   - what Edward says and does
   - how Russell uses Edward to comment on education

   [30 + 4 marks]

EXAMINATION PRACTICE ANSWERS

1. Russell presents growing up as an important theme in *Blood Brothers*. He shows Mickey at various points in his life: aged 7, 14, 18 and then in his mid-twenties. This chronological structure allows the audience to see how Mickey's outlook changes as he grows older, and the effects that social class have on Mickey's opportunities compared with his twin brother, Edward. Ultimately, Russell suggests that ageing isn't the only way a person grows up. He also emphasises that a person's experiences and responsibilities can force them to grow up faster.

   At aged 7, Mickey's childhood is largely presented as fun and carefree. Although he comes from a working-class background and his family don't always have enough to eat, he doesn't seem to let that stop him from enjoying life and playing with the other children. His underprivileged upbringing isn't a barrier between his friendship with Edward, rather it's a way for Mickey to impress Edward, who is amazed at Mickey's knowledge of the 'F' word and his supposed run-ins with the police. Russell uses immature language and childish innocence in Mickey's dialogue to remind the audience of his youth, for example, Mickey thinks the plate in Sammy's head is a piece of crockery. This amusing misunderstanding reminds the audience, that despite Mickey's bravado, he's only a child.

   When the twins reconnect aged 14, Russell presents Mickey as a typical teenager. He's awkward around girls, is self-conscious about his appearance and finds school boring. Mickey and Edward form a close bond in their teens, once again showing that their different social classes don't negatively impact their friendship, as they are able to connect by sharing experiences, such as going to the cinema, and days out at the beach and the funfair.

   Once the twins turn 18, they become more aware of the differences in their lives caused by their social class, and as a result, their friendship begins to break down. Eighteen is often considered the point of adulthood, as 18-year-olds can legally marry and purchase alcohol, and many would have left education and entered the workplace. When Mickey is 18, he gets Linda pregnant, they marry and Mickey loses his job at the factory. This sequence of events causes Mickey to grow up more quickly: he is unemployed with a family to provide for. Russell contrasts this with Edward's life aged 18: he's at university, going to parties and making friends, suggesting that he is still enjoying a life free from adult responsibilities. When Edward comes home at Christmas, Russell shows how Mickey resents Edward's freedom, as well as Edward's lack of empathy towards his unemployment. This causes a rift in the twins' friendship and the two fall out.

   Once Mickey is in his mid-twenties, the difference in maturity between him and Edward accelerates. Mickey's time in prison takes its toll on his appearance (Mickey is described as looking "*fifteen years older*") and it vastly changes his outlook on life. In his childhood, Mickey was energetic and carefree, but as an adult he is prescribed anti-depressants to help him cope with the difficulties he experiences.

   In conclusion, Russell suggests that children were often naïve about social class, and didn't understand its importance on a person's lifestyle and opportunities. However, as an adult, working-class people often had to grow up quicker than their middle-class counterparts because of the pressures of making ends meet.

2. Although it could be argued that Mickey and Edward are the main characters in *Blood Brothers*, the twins' story wouldn't be possible without the character of Mrs Lyons, so her role in the play is very important. As well as being a dramatic device who furthers the plot, Mrs Lyons also serves as a contrast to Mrs Johnstone, and highlights the difference that social class has on the lives of the two women, as well as their children.

   Firstly, Mrs Lyons instigates the action of the plot by suggesting that Mrs Johnstone give her one of the twins. This is a key moment in the play which starts a chain reaction of events which leads to the twins' downfall. Mrs Lyons convinces Mrs Johnstone to give her one of the twins using forceful language. The imperative verb 'give' in the line "*Give one to me*", presents her dialogue as a command, rather than a request. Mrs Lyons also interrupts Mrs Johnstone several times, showing her dominance in the conversation. One of the main reasons Mrs Johnstone is prepared to give one of the twins away is because Mrs Lyons is presented as Mrs Johnstone's social superior. She is from a wealthy, middle-class family, and Mrs Johnstone hopes that Edward will have a better life if he is brought up in the Lyons' family. Russell uses dialogue to reinforce Mrs Lyons as a middle-class character. She speaks in standard English, and unlike Mrs Johnstone, doesn't have a regional accent. As well as being Mrs Johnstone's social superior, Mrs Lyons is also Mrs Johnstone's employer, which puts her in a position of power, and Mrs Lyons exploits this to get what she wants: Mrs Johnstone's baby.

   After the twins are born, Mrs Johnstone has second thoughts about allowing Mrs Lyons to take the baby, but once again Mrs Lyons uses her power over Mrs Johnstone to get her own way. She invents a superstition, claiming that parted twins will die if they ever find out that they have been separated. This superstition prevents Mrs Johnstone from ever telling Mickey and Edward the truth.

   Mrs Lyons also plays an important role in providing Edward with a middle-class upbringing. The opportunities which Mrs Lyons provides for Edward eventually causes a rift between the twins when they are older, as Edward has had the opportunity to go to university while Mickey struggles to find work after he is fired from the factory.

   Throughout the play, Mrs Lyons' mental health slowly deteriorates as she becomes increasingly paranoid about Edward discovering the truth about his birth mother. Russell shows this progressive character development by showing her as an over-protective mother who tries to separate Mickey and Edward, and eventually persuading her husband to move to Skelmersdale in order to keep the truth hidden. Her mental health declines in Act Two, eventually resulting in her attacking Mrs Johnstone with a knife.

Mrs Lyons ultimately brings about the death of the twins by telling Mickey about Edward and Linda's affair. This revelation causes Mickey to hit rock bottom, and go to the Town Hall with the gun. The audience never understands Mrs Lyons' motivation for revealing the affair, but her decision to do so and its disastrous consequences present her as a villain.

In conclusion, Mrs Lyons is essential to progressing the plot at various points in the play. She also represents the middle class, and her characterisation as privileged and wealthy provides a stark contrast to Mrs Johnstone, who is struggling to get by. Mrs Lyons repeatedly takes advantage of Mrs Johnstone for her own benefit, and this, plus her decision to reveal Edward and Linda's affair, contributes to the twins' downfall.

3. Russell presents an education as one of the most important ways that a person can get ahead in society. However, since access to a 'good' education was largely reserved for those who had money, it was mainly upper- and middle-class pupils who were able to benefit from it. Russell uses the character of Edward to show that access to a 'good' education often led to well-paid professions, and he uses the character of Mickey to show how state school educations often led to low-skilled jobs which paid little. This often meant that middle-class children, like Edward, were given a better chance at success than working-class children like Mickey.

Firstly, Edward is raised in a household that places a lot of importance on education. Russell shows this by making Edward's vocabulary much more sophisticated than Mickey's, even when the boys are as young as seven. Edward is encouraged to look words up in the dictionary, whereas Mickey doesn't even know the meaning of the word 'dictionary'. The disparity between the twins' language skills becomes even more apparent as they grow older. Edward describes visiting the cinema as a "*remarkable celluloid experience*", and his elevated language choices set him apart from Mickey.

As well as contrasting the characters' use of language, Russell compares the twins' different educations by juxtaposing two scenes in Act Two. In the first scene, the audience witnesses Edward's experiences at school. Edward attends a fee-paying all-boys school. He is doing well academically, and there is talk of him going to either Oxford or Cambridge university, two of the most prestigious universities in the UK. On the other hand, Mickey attends a free co-educational state school, where he is humiliated by his teacher. Mickey's teacher comments how it's unlikely that Mickey will get a job when he's older. Even at the age of 14, Russell clearly shows how middle-class children were often given an advantage over their working-class counterparts.

Despite his private school education, Edward is presented as being book-smart, rather than someone with real-world experience. Edward gives Mickey advice about flirting from a book he has read. This suggests how well-educated people sometimes lacked experience of the real-world. This is shown again later in the play when Edward comes home from university at Christmas. When Mickey tells Edward that he's unemployed, Edward insensitively tells him to "*draw the dole, live like a bohemian*", suggesting that Edward has a romanticised, unrealistic view of unemployment. This means that he can't empathise with Mickey's situation, once again showing how his education has made him out-of-touch with reality.

When he is 18, Edward goes to university. In the 1970s-80s, typically only the upper and middle classes could afford to send their children to university, suggesting that Edward is only able to go to university due to his middle-class parents' wealth. Edward's university education helps him to get a job as a local councillor. This would have been an important role in the local community, and it gives Edward a degree of power and influence, as he is able to secure a new job and house for Mickey.

In conclusion, Russell demonstrates the importance of education by showing the differences between the twins, and the impact that their education has on their lives. In Edward's case, his middle-class upbringing afforded him a 'good' education which led to excellent employment prospects, while Mickey's education only allowed him access to menial jobs, which meant, as a low-skilled worker, he was particularly vulnerable to job cuts. Russell could be suggesting that access to education should be available to everyone, irrespective of their family's wealth, as education is one of the few ways that working-class people can break the cycle of poverty.

LEVELS-BASED MARK SCHEMES FOR EXTENDED RESPONSE QUESTIONS

Questions that require extended writing use levels. The whole answer will be marked together to determine which level it fits into, and which mark should be awarded within the level.

The descriptors below have been written in simple language to give an indication of the expectations of each level. See the AQA website for the official mark schemes used.

Level	Students' answers tend to...
6 (26–30 marks)	<ul><li>Focus on the text as conscious construct (i.e. a play written by Russell intended to have a deliberate effect).</li><li>Produce a logical and well-structured response which closely uses the text to explore their argument / interpretation.</li><li>Analyse the writer's craft by considering the effects of a writer's choice, linked closely to meanings.</li><li>Understand the writer's purpose and context.</li></ul>
5 (21–25 marks)	<ul><li>Start to think about ideas in a more developed way.</li><li>Think about the deeper meaning of a text and start to explore alternative interpretations.</li><li>Start to focus on specific elements of writer's craft, linked to meanings.</li><li>Focus more on abstract concepts, such as themes and ideas, than narrative events or character feelings.</li></ul>
4 (16–20 marks)	<ul><li>Sustain a focus on an idea, or a particular technique.</li><li>Start to consider how the text works and what the writer is doing.</li><li>Use examples effectively to support their points.</li><li>Explain the effect of a writer's method on the text, with a clear focus on it having been consciously written.</li><li>Show an understanding of ideas and themes.</li></ul>
3 (11–15 marks)	<ul><li>Explain their ideas.</li><li>Demonstrate knowledge of the text as a whole.</li><li>Show awareness of the concept of themes.</li><li>Identify the effects of a range of methods on reader.</li></ul>
2 (6–10 marks)	<ul><li>Support their comments by using references to / from the text.</li><li>Make comments that are generally relevant to the question.</li><li>Identify at least one method and possibly make some comment on the effect of it on the reader</li></ul>
1 (1–5 marks)	<ul><li>Describe the text.</li><li>Retell the narrative.</li><li>Make references to, rather than use references from, the text.</li></ul>
0 marks	Nothing worthy of credit / nothing written.

INDEX

A

accent 11, 16, 19, 40
Act One 15
Act Two 23
acts 6
addiction 29, 38
affair 29, 30, 38, 41, 42
antagonist 3
apostrophes 11
assessment objectives vi

B

boarding school 23
bus conductor 23, 24, 45

C

childish language 12, 50
chorus 3
chronological structure 7
comedy 3
conversational language 10
cyclical structure 7, 30

D

dancing 14, 23, 32
devil 13
dialect words 11
dialogue 10, 12
dole 5, 23, 27
Donna Marie 23
dramatic irony 13, 20, 21, 24

E

education 5, 7, 24, 27, 41, 46, 47
Edward 5, 8, 13, 19–22, 25, 26, 28–30, 35, 36, 40, 41, 49–51, 53
ellipsis 10
employment 5, 27, 46

F

fatal flaw 3
fate 20, 52
foreshadowing 13, 14, 19, 21, 28
freewill 53
friendship 25, 49

G

gender 18, 24, 29, 32, 34, 36, 42, 46, 55, 56
grammar school 5
growing up 20, 27, 50, 51
guns 14, 19, 28, 30
gynaecologist 17, 45

H

hyperbole 22

I

imagery 14
interruptions 10

J

juxtaposed scenes 7

L

Linda 8, 20, 21, 23–26, 28–30, 38, 40, 42, 56
Liverpool 4
locket 13, 22, 24

M

mental health 28, 35, 38, 42, 53
Mickey 3, 5, 8, 19–30, 37, 38, 40, 42, 43, 49–51, 53
middle class 4, 46, 47
milkman 15, 45
Miss Jones 27
money 46, 47
monologue 26
Monroe, Marilyn 2, 14, 28
montage 6, 26, 44
motif 14
Mr Johnstone 15, 31, 32, 56
Mr Lyons 5, 18, 22, 27, 36, 56
Mrs Johnstone 15–20, 22, 23, 25, 29–32, 34, 35, 44, 52, 55
Mrs Lyons 3, 13, 16–25, 29, 31, 32, 34, 35, 40, 52, 53, 55
musical 2

N

Narrator 6, 7, 10, 15, 17, 23, 24, 26, 30, 44, 45, 52
natural speech 10
new towns 4, 22
non-standard grammar 11

P

pauses 10
phonetic spelling 11
policeman 21
prejudice 21, 35
prologue 3, 7, 15, 30, 44
props 6, 8
protagonist 3

R

received pronunciation 11, 12, 47
regional accent 16, 19, 40
repetition 10, 12, 13
reprises 2
rhetorical questions 17, 43
rhyming couplets 10
Russell, Willy 2

S

Sammy 8, 19, 21–24, 28, 37, 38, 43
scenes 6
setting 8
simultaneous scenes 8, 28
Skelmersdale 4, 22, 23
social class 4, 20, 46, 47
soliloquies 2, 15
sound effects 6, 9
stage directions 8, 9
standard English 11, 12, 16, 19, 40, 47
structure 7, 44
superstitions 16, 19, 21, 31, 44, 52, 53

T

teacher 24, 45
Thatcher, Margaret 5
tragedy 3, 15, 53

U

university 26, 27, 41, 47, 51

W

working class 4, 46, 47

ACKNOWLEDGMENTS

The questions in this ClearRevise guide are the sole responsibility of the authors and have neither been provided nor approved by the examination board.

Every effort has been made to trace and acknowledge ownership of copyright. The publishers will be happy to make any future amendments with copyright owners that it has not been possible to contact. The publisher would like to thank the following companies and individuals who granted permission for the use of their images in this textbook.

Quotes throughout the book from © Willy Russell (1985) *Blood Brothers* Bloomsbury Publishing Plc.

Page 2 – Willy Russell © Jeremy Sutton-Hibbert / Alamy Stock Photo
Page 4 – Liverpool slum © Trinity Mirror / Mirrorpix / Alamy Stock Photo
Page 5 – Margaret Thatcher © David Fowler / Shutterstock.com
Page 8 – Mrs Johnstone and pram © Suzan Moore / Alamy Stock Photo
Page 11 – Mrs Johnstone and Mrs Lyons © Guzelian Ltd
Page 14 – Marilyn Monroe © Allstar Picture Library Ltd / Alamy Stock Photo
Page 15 – Mrs Johnstone © Trinity Mirror / Mirrorpix / Alamy Stock Photo
Page 17 – Mrs Johnstone and pram © Donald Cooper / Photostage
Page 19 – Mrs Johnstone and Mickey © PA Images / Alamy Stock Photo
Page 20 – Mickey and Edward's pact © Donald Cooper / Photostage
Page 22 – Mrs Johnson and Edward © Donald Cooper / Photostage
Page 25 – Mickey and Edward reunited © Donald Cooper / Photostage
Page 26 – Edward, Linda and Mickey © PA Images / Alamy Stock Photo
Page 27 – Mickey in the dole queue © PA Images / Alamy Stock Photo
Page 28 – Sammy and Mickey © PA Images / Alamy Stock Photo
Page 30 – Final scene © Guzelian Ltd
Page 31 – Mrs Johnstone © Suzan Moore / Alamy Stock Photo
Page 32 – Mrs Johnstone and Edward © Suzan Moore / Alamy Stock Photo
Page 34 – Mrs Lyons and Mrs Johnstone © Donald Cooper / Photostage
Page 37 – Young Mickey © Donald Cooper / Photostage
Page 40 — Young Edward © Donald Cooper / Photostage
Page 41 – Edward © Guzelian Ltd
Page 42 – Linda © Guzelian Ltd
Page 43 – Sammy © Guzelian Ltd
Page 44 – The Narrator © WENN Rights Ltd / Alamy Stock Photo
Page 44 — Edward, Linda and Mickey at the funfair © Donald Cooper / Photostage
Page 51 – Mickey and Linda's wedding © Donald Cooper / Photostage
Page 52 – Mrs Johnstone and The Narrator © PA Images / Alamy Stock Photo
Page 56 – Mickey and Linda © Donald Cooper / Photostage

All other photographs and graphics © Shutterstock.

EXAMINATION TIPS

With your examination practice, use a boundary approximation using the following table. Be aware that the grade boundaries can vary from year to year, so they should be used as a guide only.

Grade	9	8	7	6	5	4	3	2	1
Boundary	88%	79%	71%	61%	52%	43%	31%	21%	10%

1. Read the question carefully. Don't give an answer to a question that you think is appearing (or wish was appearing!) rather than the actual question.
2. Spend time reading through the question, and decide which moments from the play are the most relevant and will provide the best examples.
3. It's worth jotting down a quick plan to make sure your answer includes sufficient detail and is focused on the question. If your plan doesn't have enough material for a full response, you can plan the other question instead.
4. Start your answer with a brief introduction where you summarise the main points of your response. This can help your answer to stay on-track.
5. A discussion of Russell's methods can include his language choices, but also structural choices (such as the ordering of events), how characters develop, and what their actions tell you about their characterisation.
6. Include details from the text to support your answer. These details might be quotes, or they can be references to the text.
7. Make sure your handwriting is legible. The examiner can't award you marks if they can't read what you've written.
8. The examiner will be impressed if you can correctly use technical terms like 'dramatic irony', 'soliloquy', 'phonetic spelling', 'chronological' etc, but to get the best marks you need to explore the effect of these techniques.
9. Use linking words and phrases to show you are developing your points or comparing information, for example, "this reinforces", "this shows that" and "on the other hand". This helps to give your answer structure, and makes it easier for the examiner to award you marks.
10. If you need extra paper, make sure you clearly signal that your answer is continued elsewhere. Remember that longer answers don't necessarily score more highly than shorter, more concise answers.
11. There are 4 marks available for spelling, punctuation and grammar. Save some time at the end of the exam to read through your answer to correct any mistakes and make any improvements.

Good luck!

New titles coming soon!

Revision, re-imagined

These guides are everything you need to ace your exams and beam with pride. Each topic is laid out in a beautifully illustrated format that is clear, approachable and as concise and simple as possible.

They have been expertly compiled and edited by subject specialists, highly experienced examiners, industry professionals and a good dollop of scientific research into what makes revision most effective. Past examination questions are essential to good preparation, improving understanding and confidence.

- Hundreds of marks worth of examination style questions
- Answers provided for all questions within the books
- Illustrated topics to improve memory and recall
- Specification references for every topic
- Examination tips and techniques
- Free Python solutions pack (CS Only)

Absolute clarity is the aim.

Explore the series and add to your collection at **www.clearrevise.com**

Available from all good book shops

amazon   @pgonlinepub

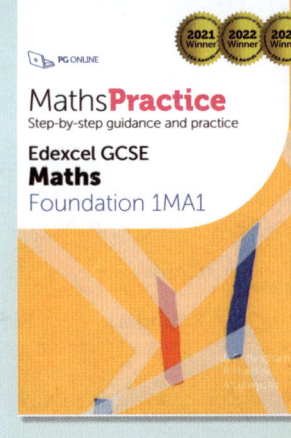

MathsPractice — Step-by-step guidance and practice
Edexcel GCSE **Maths** Foundation 1MA1

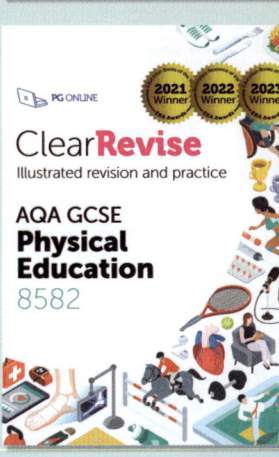

ClearRevise — Illustrated revision and practice
AQA GCSE **Physical Education** 8582

ClearRevise — AQA GCSE **English Language** 8700

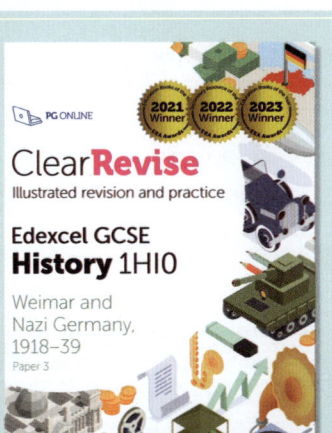

ClearRevise — Edexcel GCSE **History 1HI0** — Weimar and Nazi Germany, 1918–39 — Paper 3

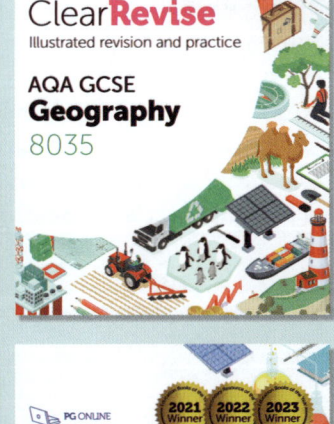

ClearRevise — AQA GCSE **Geography** 8035

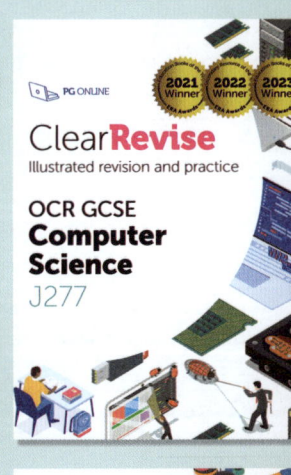

ClearRevise — OCR GCSE **Computer Science** J277

ClearRevise — AQA GCSE English Literature **Macbeth** By William Shakespeare 8702

ClearRevise — Edexcel GCSE **Business** 1BS0

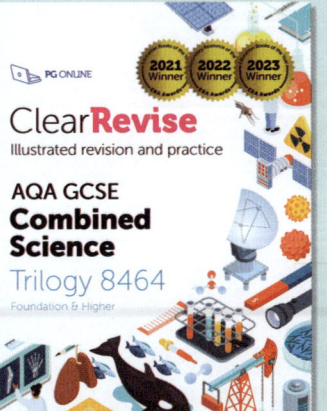

ClearRevise — AQA GCSE **Combined Science** Trilogy 8464 Foundation & Higher

ClearRevise — AQA GCSE **Design and Technology** 8552